ETERNAL STRANGERS

ETERNAL STRANGERS

Critical Views of Jews and Judaism
Through the Ages

Revised 2nd Edition

By
Thomas Dalton

Clemens & Blair, LLC
— 2025 —

CLEMENS & BLAIR, LLC

Clemens & Blair, LLC, is a non-profit educational publisher.
www.clemensandblair.com

Library of Congress Cataloging-in-Publication Data

Dalton, Thomas B.
Eternal Strangers: Critical Views of Jews and Judaism Through the Ages

Revised 2nd edition

p. cm.
Includes bibliographical references

ISBN 978-1963-1433-93
(pbk.: alk. paper)

1. Jews and Judaism
2. History, General

Printing number: 9 8 7 6 5 4 3 2 1

Printed in the United States of America on acid-free paper.

CONTENTS

ETERNAL STRANGERS

CHAPTER 1

ANTI-JEWISH MUSINGS FROM THE PRE-CHRISTIAN ERA

> This almost universal negative attitude…needs further scrutiny. Its main source must be sought in the basic fact that the Jews, in spite of their having been Europeans for so many centuries, were still considered, even by themselves, to be utter strangers.
>
> — I. Barzilay (1956: 253)

Poor Jews! Condemned by God and fate to be forever misunderstood, neglected, insulted, abused, envied, pitied—indeed, hated by all mankind. The subject of insult, calumny, slander, nay, even beatings, torture, and all manner of physical abuse. Such an unkind destiny. How did it come to this? How is it that throughout history, Jews have come to be detested, battered, and beaten down? Is it something about Jewish culture? Religion? Ethnicity? Values? And how does this long history relate to present-day abuse and hatred heaped upon Jews worldwide, and on the Jewish state?

These are important questions, given the present condition of the world and the power and influence commanded by the Jewish community generally. Part of the current animosity is based, no doubt, on the mere fact that Jews, a small minority in every nation of the world save Israel, hold grossly disproportionate power to their numbers.[1] Acting through the United States, Jews are more dominant than ever; we need only recall the statement of former Malaysian president Mahathir Mohamad, who said, "Today the Jews rule the world by proxy. They get others to fight

---

[1] The five nations with the highest Jewish percentage, apart from Israel, are: USA (2%), Canada (1%), France (0.7%), UK (0.5%), and Argentina (0.4%).

and die for them".[2] That this is problematic hardly needs to be stated. People everywhere, no matter their religious or political context, understand an elemental fact of governance: a small, wealthy, ethnic minority of people should not exert disproportionate influence in the life of a nation. That the Jews do this is undeniable, and they would be disliked on this count alone.

But there is much more to the story. Their present level of influence is unprecedented, but Jews have had access to power for millennia. As far back as 50 BC, Roman philosopher Seneca remarked critically on their influence; Jewish actions were said to disrupt "the whole world" as it was known at that time. But despite having influence and power, Jews have also been subject to numerous pogroms, banishments, and outright massacres over the centuries. Their power should have protected them, but time and again, it did not. As it happens, they had generated such hatred and resentment that mass uprisings against them proved unstoppable, even with support from the most sympathetic rulers. By recounting this history, and the observations of prominent individuals, we may better understand the Jewish phenomenon as a whole, and thus learn how to better deal with this most influential minority.

In the present work, I will trace the history of negative attitudes toward Jews and Jewish society, beginning in ancient times. The point is not to revel in abuse but to give voice to the most articulate and insightful critics of Jews—and to draw plausible conclusions.

In the academic literature, such a study would come under the heading 'history of anti-Semitism.' There is no shortage of such works; the library database WorldCat lists over 8,400 English-language books on this topic published since the year 2000. But these books—the vast majority by Jewish authors—reflect a strongly pro-Jewish bias. Consequently, the cited "anti-Semites" are nearly always portrayed as wrong, or vile, or

---

[2] As reported by FoxNews (16 October 2003). Mahathir reiterated this notion in 2016: "You look at America; it is totally dedicated to supporting Israel, even when Israel commits international crimes. ... What I said [in 2003] is that the Jews are ruling the world by proxy. If you refuse to see the evidence, then I cannot help you" (*Washington Post*, 27 June). Globally, Jews represent just 0.18% of the planet. That such a small group could "rule the world," even indirectly, will no doubt be a cause of astonishment to future historians.

misguided, or mistaken; their complaints about Jews are never valid, and the Jews themselves are virtually always exempt from blame. Jews are almost uniformly portrayed as an innocent and beleaguered people, set upon without justification by cruel and vindictive forces. Often the anti-Semitic critics are portrayed as sick individuals, sadistic in nature, even downright evil. At the very least, they are severely mentally ill. Consider this impressive statement from a recent "anatomy of anti-Semitism":

> In the 1940s and 1950s, students of anti-Semitism widely regarded that phenomenon…as a ramification of severe emotional or social disorder. They realized that Christian prejudice…could not explain the firestorm that had nearly obliterated twentieth-century European Jewry. … In the agonized post-Holocaust reassessment, … psychohistorians, psychiatrists, and psychoanalysts tended to focus on flaws in the argument that anti-Semitism sprang from christological sources. … [American postwar studies] describe anti-Semitism as an emotional disorder produced by intrapsychic tensions and sexual and social anxieties and frustrations. … Jew haters accordingly exhibit grave personality disorders. They are asocial or antisocial, alienated, isolated, inhibited, anxious, repressed, rigid, regressive, infantile, narcissistic, hostile, punitive, conformist, dependent, delusive, guilt-ridden, paranoid, irrational, aggressive, and prone to violence. (Jaher 1994: 10-12)

Frederic Jaher all but exhausts his thesaurus in seeking pejorative appellations for the insane "Jew haters." And yet we must ask ourselves: Is this rational? Were there no other causes that might have motivated the critics of Jewry? Were all the notable anti-Semites in history—and there were many, as I will show—really insane? All those prominent and brilliant individuals, by all other accounts, men of genius—were they closet lunatics? Or does the problem lie elsewhere? Is the psychosis, perhaps, resident in the Jewish personality, the Jewish psyche, the Jewish race? Is it an ethnological defense mechanism to reflect one's own deficiencies upon one's enemies?

In the following assessment of historical attitudes, I will seek common and universal themes, ones that are well-grounded and rational. Attitudes, criticisms, and other negative observations that persist over the centuries and across cultures are significant markers; they indicate a set of robust and persistent traits that are apparently embedded in the Jewish character. It is more than enlightening to examine such traits in an open and objective manner; in the present world, it is essential.

Critiques from the Ancient World

Traditionally speaking, the Jewish ethnicity traces back to Abraham, circa 1500 BC. Jews spread out around the Middle East, interacting with neighboring tribes and cultures while maintaining a strong sense of racial unity—and while practicing their early forms of usury and financial manipulation of naïve locals.[3] Within two centuries they reached Egypt, multiplied, and "the land was filled with them" (Ex 1:7). As the story goes, the pharaoh determined that "the people of Israel are too many and too mighty," and thus he had to "deal shrewdly" with them. His fear was that, in the event of some future war, the Jews might "join our enemies and fight against us"—evidently for financial or other gain. A sort of repression began but the Jews fought back; "the Egyptians were in dread of the people of Israel." A series of plagues then hit Egypt on behalf of the Jews, whereupon the pharaoh relented and they were driven out.[4] If true, this constituted the first 'anti-Semitic' act in recorded history.

Amazingly, we have independent, physical evidence for conflicts between the Egyptians and the Jews. The Amarna letters are a series of 380 clay tablets containing messages to two pharaohs, Amenhotep III and Akhenaten, dating between roughly 1360 and 1332 BC. Nine of the letters refer to one "Labayu" as a noted rebel and marauding troublemaker from Shechem,[5] in the area of present-day Israel; three other letters

---

[3] For a detailed account of this time, see G. Delaney, *The Sumerian Swindle* (2025) and *The Monsters of Babylon* (2024).

[4] The group supposedly numbered "six hundred thousand men," plus women and children (Ex 12:37). This absurdly high figure strikes an interesting comparison with the equally-absurd "6 million" allegedly killed in the Holocaust. Both numbers, centered on '6,' are purely symbolic, and not to be taken literally.

[5] Mentioned in the Old Testament; see 1 Kings 12:1.

are from Labayu himself. In letter EA 244, Biridiya of Megidda complains to Akhenaten as follows:

> May the king, my lord, know that…Labayu has waged war against me. We are thus unable to do the [harvesting], because of Labayu. … May the king save [Megidda] lest Labayu seize it. … Labayu has no other purpose; he seeks simply the seizure of Meggida. (Moran 1987: 298)

Significantly, Labayu and his two sons were in evident collaboration with "the Habiru" (or 'Apiru'), which some scholars have identified as "the Hebrews." Paul Johnson (1987: 23) suggests that Labayu and sons were the "coreligionists and racial kin" of the Jews enslaved in Egypt. Labayu "caused great difficulties for the Egyptian authorities and their allies; as with all other Habiru, he was…a nuisance." And insolent; in EA 252, Labayu threatens to "bite the hand" of Akhenaten; "how can I show deference?" he complains. He is furthermore constantly trying to refute his image as a rebel. Such impudence seems to have given the Habiru/Hebrews an early and rather nasty reputation.

Even if the Exodus was pure fiction, we do have concrete evidence of a people called "Israel" by 1200 BC. The 1896 discovery of an engraved stone in east-central Egypt, known as the Merneptah Stele, brought to light a cryptic but telling line: "Israel is laid waste, and his seed is not." We don't know the context, but evidently certain Egyptians came into conflict with "Israel" and defeated them badly—to the point that they were virtually exterminated (at least, locally). This event might be considered the second historical action against the Jews, and the first to be definitively dated. In any case, the Jews apparently established themselves in Palestine, creating the unified Kingdom of David by 1000 BC. Shortly thereafter they built their first temple (Solomon's Temple) in Jerusalem.[6]

Another negative incident occurred around the year 850 BC, one that was recorded on the Tel Dan Stele, recently discovered in northern Israel. On this stone, a King Hazael boasts of his victory over the Israeli

---

[6] This temple was destroyed in 586 BC by Babylonian king Nebuchadnezzar. The Second Temple was built in 516 BC, which in turn was destroyed by the Romans in 70 AD; the western ('Wailing') wall is all that remains today.

kings and the "House of David." Evidently the Jews had invaded his father's land, and Hazael had subsequently exacted his revenge. As before,
an apparently aggressive and hostile Jewish people attacked their neighbors, and paid a price for their belligerence.

The next detailed account of "Jew hatred" is documented later in the
Old Testament, in the Book of Esther. Esther was the alleged Jewish
queen of Persian King Xerxes (Ahasuerus), circa 475 BC. The king's
second-in-command, Haman, grew to hate the Jews because of their insolence, especially that of Esther's cousin Mordecai. Consequently, "Haman
sought to destroy all the Jews" (Esther 3:6). He issued directives "to destroy, to slay, and to annihilate all Jews," and built a monstrous gallows,
50 cubits high (about 25 m, or some 80 feet), just to hang Mordecai.
Through various trickery, Esther turned the tables, and Haman himself
ended up on the gallows.[7] This of course is the Jewish version of events,
and we have no independent account of this story, but still, it is reasonable to assume some factual basis at its core. And it shows that the Jews
have been able to inure themselves to powerful figures for millennia.

Yet another anti-Jewish incident occurred in the year 410 BC, in
which the Egyptian military commander Vidranga attacked and destroyed the Jewish temple at Elephantine, on the upper Nile.[8] With these
early events, we find the emergence of a trend: where the Jews settled
amongst other peoples, they seem to have made enemies.

For roughly the first millennium of their existence, no outside writers made note of the Hebrew tribe—or at least, no writings have survived. We have only the internal, Old Testament Jewish account of
things, which is no doubt glorified and exaggerated in turn. Of interest
here is how the outsiders, the non-Jews, viewed them when they did
begin to take notice.

The first to comment were the Greeks. Through seafaring trade and
imperial expansion, they came into contact with many groups of the eastern Mediterranean, including Egyptians, Phoenicians, Syrians, and Jews.
The earliest direct references come from Theophrastus and Hecateus of
Abdera, but there are two preceding and suggestive passages from Plato.

---

[7] The Jews then went on a rampage, and with the king's backing, killed over
75,000 of their "enemies" (9:16). This happy event is celebrated today in the
Jewish holiday of Purim.
[8] For a detailed account of this event, see Schafer (1997: 132-138).

The first is in *Republic*, dated circa 375 BC. Amidst a discussion of justice in the polis, Plato identifies three social classes: rulers, auxiliaries (military), and the "money-makers" (businessmen). He then compares these qualities to neighboring cultures, observing that "the love of money …is conspicuously displayed by the Phoenicians and Egyptians" (436a). It is likely that, by 'Phoenicians,' Plato means to include the Jews, even though they were not yet identified by that name. At that time, there was general confusion about the various tribes of that region, but the Hebrews were the dominant power in Phoenicia.[9] Regardless, it is striking that the people there were widely known as lovers of money.

A second and related reference comes from Plato's final work (ca. 350 BC), *Laws*. In Book V he discusses the virtue and value of mathematics, under the condition that we "expel the spirit of pettiness and greed" (747c) that would otherwise invite abuse of that skill. If a teacher fails to do this, he will have inadvertently produced a "twister," a dangerously corrupt person—as has happened "in the case of the Egyptians and Phoenicians, and many other races whose approach to wealth and life in general shows a narrow-minded outlook." This could reflect a general sense of Athenian elitism, but it is interesting that Plato again cites those two groups specifically.

But it is not until roughly 310 BC that we find the first explicit reference to the Jews, by Aristotle's chief pupil Theophrastus. It seems he had a concern about one of their customs:

> [T]he Syrians, of whom the Jews (*Ioudaioi*) constitute a part, also now sacrifice live victims. … They were the first to institute sacrifices both of other living beings and of themselves.

---

[9] Emilio Gabba notes that, at that time, "the distinctions between the various peoples of the Syrian and Phoenician regions" had yet to emerge. Herodotus (484–425 BC) refers to the "Phoenicians" and the "Syrians of Palestine" as tribes that have adopted the practice of circumcision. And the Jewish writer Josephus (ca. 37–100 AD) remarks that the Jews "spoke the Phoenician language." See Gabba (1984: 615, 618). Delaney (2025, chap. 14) is certain that the Phoenicians were Jews. Wells (1922: 286) writes: "To Phoenicians after the falls of Tyre and Carthage, conversion to Judaism must have been particularly easy and attractive. Their language was closely akin to Hebrew. It is possible that the great majority of African and Spanish Jews are really of Phoenician origin." As a final observation, I would note that Homer called the Phoenicians "swindlers" (*Odyssey* 15.465).

The Greeks, he added, would have "recoiled from the entire business".[10] The victims—animal and human—were not eaten, but burnt as "whole offerings" to their God, and were "quickly destroyed." The philosopher was clearly repelled by this Jewish tradition.

Remarkably, Theophrastus' word for 'whole burnt offering' is "holocaust" (*holokautountes*)—meaning a complete burning (*holos-kaustos*). Thus the very first Greek reference to Jews *also* includes the very first reference to a "holocaust." Fate works in strange ways indeed.[11]

It was around that time that the Macedonian general Ptolemy I came to rule Egypt. His military, for various reasons, could not conscript Egyptian citizens, and so a mercenary army was necessary. Fortunately, Ptolemy had a ready supply at hand in the Jews. Gabba (1984: 635) relates that the king employed 30,000 Jews, chosen from among his many prisoners of war. "Well paid and highly trustworthy, they served to keep the native population at bay, and the natives apparently retaliated against them from time to time."

This, in addition to the cultural and religious quirks, was another basis for indigenous animosity towards Jews. It anticipates the similar use of Jewry by future leaders of Europe and Russia—with comparable results. But again, this incident is revealing. It is understandable to want to get out of prison, but one must wonder at the evident readiness of the Jews to side *with their enemies*, for pay, and to do so enthusiastically, with little compunction.

Hecateus, working somewhat after Theophrastus, wrote the first text dedicated to the subject: *On the Jews*.[12] Two fragments survive, one by the Jewish writer Josephus and the other by Diodorus. Generally speaking, both fragments are sympathetic to the Jews, and thus it is striking that the latter includes this observation on the story of the Exodus:

---

[10] In Stern (1974: 10).

[11] References to "burnt offering" (*olah*) occur repeatedly in the Old Testament, including in Genesis: "Noah built an alter to the Lord…and offered burnt offerings on the altar" (Gen 8:20). And again in Gen 22:2: "Take your son…and offer him there as a burnt offering upon one of the mountains…" By one estimate, there are 289 occurrences of the phrase in the OT.

[12] According to Josephus, *Contra Apionem*, I.183.

[A]s a consequence of having been driven out [of Egypt], Moses introduced a way of life which was, to a certain extent, misanthropic and hostile to foreigners" (*apanthropon tina kai mixoxenon bion*).[13]

One can certainly understand the anger of any people who have been driven from their place of residence. But why should this translate into *misanthropy*—that is, hatred of mankind in general? It is as if the Jews took out their anger on the rest of humanity. Jewish misanthropy, in fact, is rooted in the Old Testament and thus was well-established long before the time of Hecateus; he was not mistaken.

But there is a second question here: Why were the Jews driven out? Egyptian high priest Manetho (ca. 250 BC) tells of a group of "lepers and other polluted persons," 80,000 in number, who were exiled from Egypt and found residence in Judea. There they established Jerusalem and built a large temple. Manetho comments that the Jews kept to themselves, as it was their law "to interact with none save those of their own confederacy." As the story continues, the Jews ("Solymites") marshaled allies from amongst other 'polluted' persons, returned to Egypt, and temporarily conquered a large territory. When in power they treated the natives "impiously and savagely," "set[ting] towns and villages on fire, pillaging the temples and mutilating images of the gods without restraint," and roasting ('holocausting') the animals held sacred by the locals.[14] The degree of truthfulness here is uncertain, but once again it is reasonable to assume some factual basis.

Into the Roman Era

The Seleucid (Macedonian) king Antiochus IV Epiphanes ruled over the territory of Judea in the early second century BC. Internal Jewish disputes elevated to a general insurrection, angering him. His army invaded Jerusalem in 168 BC, killing many Jews and plundering their great (second) temple. Greek philosopher Posidonius adds that, upon seizing the temple, Epiphanes freed a Greek citizen who was being held captive,

---

[13] In Gabba (1984: 629).
[14] In Stern (1974: 82-83).

only to be fattened up for sacrifice, and eaten. This was allegedly an annual ritual.[15] He further remarks that the Jews worshipped the head of an ass, having placed one of solid gold in their temple. Nonetheless, within a few years, the Jews prevailed in the so-called Maccabean Revolt, reestablishing Jewish rule over Judea—a situation that would last until the Romans invaded in 63 BC.

The decline of the Seleucids coincided with Roman ascent. Rome was still technically a republic in the second century BC, but its power and influence were rapidly growing. As usual, Jews were attracted to the seat of power and migrated to Rome in significant numbers. And as usual, they came to be hated. By 139 BC, the Roman praetor Hispalus found it necessary to expel them from the city: "The same Hispalus banished the Jews from Rome, who were attempting to hand over their own rites to the Romans, and he cast down their private alters from public places".[16] In even this short passage, one senses a Roman Jewry who were disproportionately prominent, obtrusive, even 'pushy.'

Perhaps in part because of this incident, and in light of the Maccabean revolt some 30 years earlier, the Seleucid king Antiochus VII Sidetes was advised in 134 BC to exterminate the Jews. Referring to the account by Posidonius, Gabba (1984: 645) explains that the king was called on

> to destroy the Jews, for they alone among all peoples refused all relations with other races, and saw everyone as their enemy; their forbears, impious and cursed by the gods, had been driven out of Egypt. The counselors [cited] the Jews' hatred of all mankind, sanctioned by their very laws, which forbade them to share their table with a Gentile or give any sign of benevolence.

This is a telling statement; if the Jews "alone among all peoples" displayed a kind of misanthropy, this suggests something unique and distinctly pernicious among the tribe of Hebrews. It was not that everyone was suspicious of others; rather, the Jews displayed a special and striking sort of

---

[15] Josephus, *Contra Apionem*, II.79, 91-97. See also Stern (1974: 146-147).
[16] Cited in Valerius Maximus, *Facta et Dicta* (1.3.3). In an alternate account, the Jews were only confined to their homes, not banished.

malevolence toward others that Posidonius found nowhere else. Needless to say, Sidetes did not heed his counselors' advice.

Two or three decades after Posidonius, around the year 75 BC, prominent speaker and teacher Apollonius Molon wrote the first book to explicitly confront the Hebrew tribe, *Against the Jews*. From his early years in Caria and Rhodes, he would likely have had direct contact with them and thus was able to write from personal experience. Molon referred to Moses as a "charlatan" and "imposter," viewing the Jews as "the very vilest of mankind".[17] Josephus adds the following:

> [Molon] has scattered [his accusations] here and there all over his work, reviling us in one place as atheists and misanthropes, in another reproaching us as cowards, whereas elsewhere, on the contrary, he accuses us of temerity and reckless madness. He adds that we are the most witless of all barbarians, and are consequently the only people who have contributed no useful invention to civilization.[18]

The Jews are 'atheists' in the sense that they reject the Roman gods. The 'misanthrope' charge recurs, having first appeared in Hecateus. But the complaints of cowardice, villainy, and recklessness are new, as is the statement that the Jews have contributed nothing of value to civilization. The rhetoric is clearly heating up.

In 63 BC, a momentous event: Roman general Pompey takes Palestine. For most residents of the region, this was nothing to be feared, and in fact promised to bring significant improvements in many areas of life. After all, the Romans frequently granted citizenship to those they conquered, and certainly brought many advances in standard of living. But as the formerly dominant force in Judea, the Jews would have been particularly incensed. And now the Romans had to face their wrath directly, in the form of an on-going insurrection.

Thus it is unsurprising that we find a quick succession of anti-Jewish comments by notable Romans. Five are of interest, beginning with Cicero. In the year 59 BC, he gave a speech, now titled *Pro Flacco*,

---

[17] In Stern (1974: 155-156).
[18] In Stern (1974: 155). Cf. *Contra Apionem*, II.148.

that offered a defense of L. V. Flaccus, a Roman propraetor in Asia, who was charged with embezzling Jewish gold destined for Jerusalem. Strikingly, Cicero begins by noting the power and influence of the Jews:

> You know what a big crowd it is, how they stick together, how influential they are in informal assemblies. So I will speak in a low voice so that only the jurors may hear; for those are not wanting who would incite them against me and against every respectable man.[19]

Shades of the Israel Lobby! Certainly there is a tone of sarcasm here, but it is rather shocking that Cicero, speaking near the height of Roman power, should voice this concern at all—if even as a mock concern.

He continues on, noting that the senate had a long-standing policy of restricting gold exports, and that Flaccus was only enforcing this rule, not withholding the gold for himself. Here was his downfall: "But to resist this barbaric superstition (*barbarae superstitioni*) was an act of firmness, to defy the crowd of Jews (*Iudaeorum*) when sometimes in our assemblies they were hot with passion…" All the gold is accounted for, Cicero hastens to add. The whole trial "is just an attempt to fix odium on him" (recalling present-day attempts to smear 'anti-Semites'). The Jewish religion is "at variance with the glory of our empire, the dignity of our name, the customs of our ancestors." That the gods stand opposed to this tribe "is shown by the fact that it has been conquered, let out for taxes, made a slave"—so much for the so-called chosen people of God.[20]

Ten years later, Diodorus Siculus wrote his *Historical Library*. Among other things, it recounts the Exodus:

> [T]he ancestors of the Jews had been driven out of all Egypt as men who were impious and detested by the gods. For by way of purging the country of all persons who had white or leprous marks on their bodies had been assembled and driven across the border, as being under a curse; the refugees had occupied the territory round about Jerusalem,

---

[19] In Stern (1974: 197).

[20] In another work, *De Provinciis Consularibus*, Cicero adds that the Jews were a "people born to be slaves"; see Stern, p. 203.

and having organized the nation of Jews had made their hatred of mankind into a tradition… (HL 34,1)

The *Library* then includes a retelling of Antiochus Epiphanes' takeover
of the Jewish temple in 168—the same event found in the earlier work of
Posidonius. But this is no mere duplication; it demonstrates an ac-
ceptance and endorsement of that account. Here, though, it is Antiochus
Epiphanes, not his successor Sidetes, that was urged "to wipe out completely the race of Jews, since they alone, of all nations, avoided dealings
with any other people and looked upon all men as their enemies (*polemi-
ous hypolambanein pantas)*".[21] Again we find this telling statement:
"they alone, of all nations." It's not that the Romans found fault with everyone. Rather, the Jews were singled out, of all the ethnicities that the
Romans encountered; Jews alone seemed to be uniquely disposed toward
hatred of their fellow men.

Upon entering the temple Antiochus finds a statue of a bearded man
on an ass—Moses, the one "who had ordained for the Jews their misanthropic and lawless customs." Antiochus' advisors were "shocked by
such hatred directed against all mankind," and therefore "strongly urged
[him] to make an end of the race completely." In his magnanimity, if not
his wisdom, he declined.

The great lyric poet Horace (65-8 BC) wrote his *Satires* (Latin:
Sermones) in 35 BC, exploring Epicurean philosophy and the meaning of
happiness. At one point, though, he makes a passing comment on the
apparently notorious proselytizing ability of the Roman Jews—in particular their tenaciousness in winning over others. Horace is in the midst of
attempting to persuade the reader of his point of view: "and if you do not
wish to yield, then a great band of poets will come to my aid…and, just
like the Jews, we will compel you to concede to our crowd" (*Satires*
I.4.143). Their power must have been legendary or he would not have
made such an allusion.

The fourth reference comes from Ptolemy the Historian, circa 25
BC. In his *History of Herod,* he discusses the different ethnicities of Palestine, and comments on the people known as 'Idumaeans' (or 'Edom-
ites'), a tribe living in the southern desert region of present-day Israel.

---

[21] Cf. Stern, p. 183.

They were defeated by the Hebrews in 125 BC and absorbed into the Jewish nation. Ptolemy notes that the original Jews are ethnically—that is, genetically—distinct. This is in noted contrast to the 'converted' Idumaeans, who suffered genital mutilation as a mark of their incorporation:

> Jews and Idumaeans differ... Jews are those who are so by origin and nature. The Idumaeans, on the other hand, were not originally Jews, but Phoenicians and Syrians—having been subjugated by the Jews and having been forced to undergo circumcision, so as to be counted among the Jewish nation...[22]

If the Jews are distinct by "origin" (*arches*) and "nature" (*physichoi*), this clearly points to a racial definition, in addition to the obvious religious designation. The debate about the religious vs. ethnic characterization of the Jews is ancient indeed.[23]

Ptolemy was one of the first, outside the Bible, to comment on the Jewish practice of circumcision. He does not offer his opinion on it, but clearly sees it as a brutality when inflicted upon unwilling males, presumably even adolescents and adults.[24]

---

[22] In Stern (1974: 356).

[23] Jewish racial identity has been built up over centuries due to a quasi-eugenic inbreeding strategy, in which the most learned males (rabbis) were granted preferential reproductive rights. Mating outside the racial group has always been minimal, resulting in a relatively 'pure' ethnicity. As a result, Jews form a distinct and genetically identifiable subgroup—hence, a true 'race.' This is true for Ashkenazi (about 75% of all Jews), Sephardic, and Mizrahi Jews. For some relevant genetic studies, see Seldin et al (2006), Atzmon et al (2010), Carmi et al (2014), and Lazaridis et al (2014). Also, Harry Ostrer (2012) argues that Jews have a distinctive genetic signature and hence that there is a "biological basis of Jewishness." Apart from establishing a genetic uniqueness, inbreeding has led to a variety of inherited 'Jewish' diseases. Jewish journalist Jon Entine writes that "Today, Jews remain identifiable in large measure by the 40 or so diseases we disproportionately carry, the inescapable consequence of inbreeding." Such a situation may also help to explain pervasive psychological pathologies that may be uniquely prevalent in Jews. Regarding a Biblical basis for inbreeding and against intermarriage with other ethnicities, see Ex (34:11-12) and Deut (7:1-3).

[24] This is an ancient custom, apparently originating in Egypt and neighboring tribes of the eastern Mediterranean. Herodotus, circa 425 BC, wrote that "the Egyptians practice circumcision" (*Histories* II.36), and that "the Phoenicians [i.e.

The last commentator of the pre-Christian era is Lysimachus. Writing circa 20 BC, he offers a variation on the Exodus story, placing it in the reign of the pharaoh Bocchoris (or Bakenranef) of 720 BC. On his version, the Jews, "afflicted with leprosy, scurvy, and other maladies," sought refuge in Egyptian temples. The oracles advised Bocchoris to cleanse the temples, to banish the impious and impure, and "to pack the lepers into sheets of lead and sink them in the ocean"—which he did. The exiled ones, led by Moses, were instructed to "show goodwill to no man," to offer "the worst advice" to others, and to overthrow any temples or sanctuaries they might come upon. Arriving in Judea, "they maltreated the population, and plundered and set fire to the [local] temples." They then built a town called Hierosolyma (Jerusalem), and referred to themselves as Hierosolymites.[25] If indeed they persecuted the indigenous population, one can see in this a distant predecessor to the current Israeli atrocities in Palestine.

*****

The charge of *misanthropy*, or hatred of mankind, is significant and merits further discussion. It has recurred several times already—in Hecateus, Posidonius, Molon, Diodorus, and now Lysimachus. This is striking because the Romans were notably tolerant of other sects and religions, owing in part to their polytheistic worldview. A society of many gods implicitly recognizes religious diversity; if there are many such beings, who can claim complete knowledge of the divine realm? Monotheism, in contrast, claims exclusive and absolute knowledge; one God implies one ultimate truth, and other religions with other gods are necessarily false. Thus it is reasonable to assume that the Jews, as the first monotheists of the Middle East, did not reciprocate Roman tolerance. In fact, this seems

---

the Jews] learned the practice from Egypt" (II.104). In the New Testament it is cited as a distinguishing marker between the circumcised Jews and non-circumcised Gentiles. Technically, of course, it is little more than male genital mutilation, on par with (though less harmful than) the detested female version. Circumcision is still widespread to this day. In the US, rates have traditionally hovered around 55%, though it has dropped sharply in recent years—down to about 33% of all males.

[25] Stern (1974: 384-385).

to have been a general rule throughout history: religious intolerance de-rives from the monotheistic fundamentalists (Jews, Christians, Muslims), not the polytheists or religious pluralists.

In the case of the Jews, though, monotheistic arrogance was com-bined with racial distinctness and other cultural characteristics, resulting in a deeply-embedded misanthropic streak. In the Jewish mindset, non-Jews are lesser beings, almost animals, certainly not "chosen" by God, and therefore are to be viewed with contempt. They are to be ruled over; and if they resist, to be killed. This is the repeated message that we find in the Old Testament. For example:

- Let peoples serve you, and nations bow down to you. (Gen 27:29)
- I [God] will put the dread and fear of you upon the peoples that are under the whole heaven, [the Gentiles] shall tremble and be in anguish because of you. (Deut 2:25)
- Moreover, the Lord your God will send the hornet among them [the Gentiles] until even the survivors who hide from you have perished. … The Lord your God will drive out those [Gentile] nations before you, little by little. … But the Lord your God will deliver them over to you, throwing them into great confusion un-til they are destroyed. He will give their kings into your hand, and you will wipe out their names from under heaven. No one will be able to stand up against you; you will destroy them. (Deut 7:20-25)
- You shall rule over many nations… They shall be afraid of you. (Deut 15:6, 28:10)
- Those who strive against you shall be as nothing and shall per-ish. (Isaiah 41:11)
- You shall eat the wealth of [Gentile] nations. (Isaiah 61:6)

Lest we think this was merely an ancient Jewish attitude, we need only look to the present-day Middle East and the conflict in Palestine, where Jewish misanthropy and cruelty are on full display for all to see. One need only recall the words of a prominent rabbi from 2010: "The Goyim [non-Jews] were born only to serve us. Without that, they have no place in the world. They will work, they will plow, they will reap. We will sit like an effendi and eat" (*Jerusalem Post*, 18 Oct 2010). Is this not explicit misanthropy? And do these texts not express the essential Jewish worldview?

Jews thus have little concern or true compassion for other races—unless, of course, it serves to benefit them. Authentic altruism seems to be all but lacking. Even towards those who have shown them good will, good will is not returned. Rather, Jews have, historically, abused and oppressed anyone, any non-Jews, if it was in their interests. For centuries, Jews have been willing to serve as executors or enforcers of state power (when they had none of their own), with little evident regard for adverse effects on others. In one of the earliest Bible stories, Joseph, son of Jacob, finds favor with the Egyptian pharaoh, only to use his power to exploit the local farmers when a famine strikes.[26] Later we read of the Jews' ruthless slaughter of the Canaanites, and their brutal support for Ptolemy I in Egypt (cited above).

Jewish hatred of humanity is not simply one of the earliest but also one of the most persistent criticisms. This is bad enough in its own right, but it becomes even worse when combined with another core Jewish mandate: *to rule the world*. As we see in the above quotations, the Jewish God, Yahweh, grants the Hebrews the right to dominate, to own, and to consume the Earth. Misanthropy, combined with a biblical mandate of dominion or world rule, creates a highly pernicious and deadly form of *Jewish supremacism*: Jews, in their own self-image, are superior to all other peoples, whom they detest, and therefore Jews are justified in dominating and ruling over them.

This is the essence of the Jewish Problem over the centuries; it is the key to understanding how Jews think and act. Jewish supremacism was obscured for many centuries, primarily because of the Jews' small relative numbers and their relative lack of power. Throughout this time, only the most perceptive observers were able to discern its action. But in the past 200 years or so, it has become apparent to many, and since roughly the year 2000, it is now evident to all. Many prominent commentators over the centuries have observed this especially pernicious trait. And it explains much of Jewish behavior through the present day.

---

[26] See Genesis 47.

CHAPTER 2
OF ROMANS AND CHRISTIANS

The turn of the millennium was significant on several counts. Rome had formally become an empire under Augustus, as of 27 BC. Jesus of Nazareth was (allegedly) born around 3 BC. Jewish philosopher Philo was active at this time, as was the great Roman writer and thinker Seneca. Another contemporary was perhaps the most notorious 'anti-Semite' of that age, Apion. His notoriety derives not so much from his accusations—which were mostly preexisting ones—but instead for his renown amongst the upper classes of Alexandrian society, and because the Jewish writer Josephus elected to title one of his own books *Against Apion* (*Contra Apionem*). As Stern (1974: 390) says, "Apion was a rather popular writer," and thus it is no wonder "that it was Apion, among all the anti-Semitic Graeco-Egyptian writers, whom Josephus chose as his main target." A sample of the criticisms laid by Apion in his book *Against the Jews* includes:

- The leprosy-ridden Exodus story.
- An etymology of the Jewish term 'Sabbath' that derives from 'tumors of the groin.'
- Numerous tales of Jewish foolishness or naiveté.
- Well-deserved mistreatment by Cleopatra (withholding of corn during a regional famine, and various conflicts with the Jewish king Herod).
- Jews' failure to erect statues of the emperors.
- Tendency "to show no goodwill to a single alien, above all to Greeks."
- Unjust laws.
- "Erroneous" religious practices.
- Failure to produce any geniuses in the arts or crafts.
- Not eating pork.
- Circumcision.

Apion evidently supplied something of a catalog of complaints against the Jews, adding a few of his own in the process. This again suggests a lengthy and persistent history of well-deserved criticism.

Additionally, there were solid, objective reasons for the Roman public to be wary in that first century. With the Roman incorporation of Judea in 63 BC, Jews flocked to the imperial capitol in ever-greater numbers. Once again, the authorities took action. Emperor Tiberius expelled them in the year 19 AD:

> He abolished foreign cults, especially the Egyptian and Jewish rites, compelling all who were addicted to such superstitions to burn their religious vestments... [Other Jews] were banished from the city, on pain of slavery for life if they did not obey.[1]

The expulsion did not last. Eleven years later, the head of the Praetorian Guard, Sejanus, found reason to oppose them again. According to the Jewish writer Philo, Sejanus raised a series of "accusations which had been brought against the Jews who were dwelling in Rome," because "[he] was desirous to destroy our nation".[2] We know few details, but this action too seems to have had little lasting effect.

Just three years later, in the year 33, a young Jew named Jesus was crucified. This would have monumental consequence for Jewish relations with the rest of the world, though it would be several decades before they began to play out.[3]

In 38, another pogrom, nominally worse than that of Sejanus, was initiated by A. A. Flaccus in Alexandria.[4] Philo describes this event in great detail in his work *Flacco*. His many advisors urged Flaccus to curry favor with Rome "by abandoning and denouncing all the Jews" of Alexandria, lest they gain too much power. The advisors encouraged random attacks on synagogues and Jewish property, hoping that the pogrom would spread to other lands. Flaccus ended Jewish privilege, reducing

---

[1] As recorded by Suetonius; see Stern (1974: 112-113).
[2] Philo, "On the embassy to Gaius," XXIV, 159.
[3] Nietzsche offers a particularly fascinating account of the Jewish origins of Christianity; see Dalton (2010).
[4] No apparent relation to the L. V. Flaccus defended by Cicero.

them to stateless "foreigners and aliens." He terminated their right to run businesses, and money-lenders lost what they had loaned. His men drove the Jews out of most areas of the city, confining them in one small quarter, thus effectively forming the first Jewish ghetto in history. Finally, Flaccus "allowed anyone who was inclined to proceed to exterminate the Jews as prisoners of war."

So confined, they were set upon by a murderous crowd. In a long passage that ranks with the best tales of the Holocaust, Philo describes the massacre:

> And then, being immediately seized by those who had excited the seditious multitude against them, [the Jews] were treacherously put to death, and then were dragged along and trampled underfoot by the whole city, and completely destroyed, without the least portion of them being left which could possibly receive burial; and in this way their enemies, who in their savage madness had become transformed into the nature of wild beasts, slew them and thousands of others with all kinds of agony and tortures, and newly invented cruelties, for wherever they met with or caught sight of a Jew, they stoned him, or beat him with sticks, not at once delivering their blows upon mortal parts, lest they should die speedily, and so speedily escape from the sufferings which it was their design to inflict upon them.
>
> Some persons even, going still great and greater lengths in the iniquity and license of their barbarity, disdained all blunter weapons, and took up the most efficacious arms of all, fire and iron, and slew many with the sword, and destroyed not a few with flames. And the most merciless of all their persecutors in some instances burnt whole families, husbands with their wives, and infant children with their parents, in the middle of the city, sparing neither age nor youth, nor the innocent helplessness of infants. And when they had a scarcity of fuel, they collected faggots of green wood, *and slew them by the smoke* rather than by fire, contriving a still more miserable and protracted death for those unhappy people, so that their bodies laid about promiscu-

ously in every direction half burnt, a grievous and most miserable sight.

And if some of those who were employed in the collection of sticks were too slow, they took their own furniture, of which they had plundered them, to burn their persons, robbing them of their most costly articles, and burning with them things of the greatest use and value, which they used as fuel instead of ordinary timber.

Many men too, who were alive, they bound by one foot, fastening them round the ankle, and thus they dragged them along and bruised them, leaping on them, designing to inflict the most barbarous of deaths upon them, and then when they were dead they raged no less against them with interminable hostility, and inflicted still heavier insults on their persons, dragging them, I had almost said, through all the alleys and lanes of the city, until the corpse, being lacerated in all its skin, and flesh, and muscles from the inequality and roughness of the ground, all the previously united portions of his composition being torn asunder and separated from one another, was actually torn to pieces. (*Flaccus*, IX, 65-71)

Note the italicized passage; this would be the first recorded incident in history of the gassing of Jews.[5]

But Flacco was unable to finish his evil deed. In time-honored Jewish fashion, the Alexandrian Jews appealed to higher authorities in Rome and managed to get Flacco arrested, exiled, and ultimately killed. All this, however, is according to Philo—not an unbiased observer. The fact that we have no objective confirmation of this story suggests that it is exaggerated and over-dramatized.

Whether or not the Alexandrian pogrom occurred as described, there is no doubt that it was a time of on-going friction between the Jews, on the one hand, and the Greeks and Egyptians on the other. Three years later, in the year 41, Emperor Claudius issued his third edict, the *Letter to*

---

[5] For more on the history of such gassings, see Dalton (2020).

the Alexandrians, in which he admonishes all parties for the strife; but the Jews are singled out for rebuke. They have been allowed to live "in a city which is not their own," and "they possess an abundance of all good things," but must not exacerbate the situation by continually inviting in more Jews. In abusing their privileges and sowing discord, the Jews could be blamed for "fomenting a general plague which infests the whole world" (*koinen teina tes oikoumenes noson exegeirontas*). The threat itself is not so harsh, but what is striking here is the use, for the first time, of the notorious 'biological' imagery against the Jews. To suggest that they are a plague infesting the whole world is to suggest a subhuman people, one that is potentially in need of 'disinfection.' Such talk recurs periodically in the following centuries, and it foreshadows the much more ominous language of the 19th and 20th centuries.

Back in Rome, anti-Jewish actions continued. In 49, Claudius once again had to expel them. In a fascinating line from Suetonius circa the year 120, we find mention of one 'Chrestus' (Latin: *Chresto*) as the leader of the rabble; this would (likely) be one of the first non-Jewish references to Jesus. "Since the Jews constantly made disturbances at the instigation of Chrestus, [Claudius] expelled them from Rome" (*Divus Claudius*, 25:4).[6] This is an important first distinction, between the so-called Christian Jews—all early Christians *were* ethnic Jews—and the traditional Judaic ones.

In spite of all this, the beleaguered tribe still earned no sympathy. The great philosopher Seneca commented on them in his work *On Superstition*, circa 60. He was appalled not only with their "superstitious" religious beliefs, but more pragmatically with their astonishing influence in Rome and around the known world, despite repeated pogroms and banishments. Seneca first derides the Jews as lazy because they dedicate every seventh day to God: "their practice [of the Sabbath] is inexpedient, because by introducing one day of rest in every seven they lose in idleness almost a seventh of their life…".[7] "Meanwhile," he adds,

> the customs of this accursed race (*sceleratissima gens*) have gained such influence that they are now received

---

[6] In Stern (1974: 113).
[7] In Stern (1974: 431).

throughout all the world. The vanquished have given laws
to their victors.

Seneca is clearly indignant—and perhaps even jealous—at their reach.
This little race, this *accursed* race, has earned sway across vast reaches of
the civilized world. Not so much a threat, it would seem, but rather a sign
of the gradual decay of the mighty *imperium Romanum*.

Writing at the same time as Seneca, Petronius took a quick stab at
two Jewish customs: abstinence from pork, and circumcision. In his *Sa-
tyricon* he writes, "The Jew may worship his pig-god and clamor in the
ears of high heaven, but unless he also cuts back his foreskin with the
knife, he shall [not truly live as a Jew]" (frag. 37).[8]

Then came the historic Jewish revolt in Judea, during the years 66
to 70. I won't recount the details here but simply note that it ended in
Roman victory and the destruction of the second temple in Jerusalem. It
was a major defeat for the Hebrews, but they would continue to resist for
decades. Two further major uprisings occurred in 115 and 130, both end-
ing in defeat as well. Nonetheless, Jewish influence and the nascent
Judeo-Christian theology continued to grow, and to weaken the philosophical foundations of the Empire.

Tacitus and the Second Century AD

The second century of the Christian era saw a continued string of critical
comments, for the most part reiterations of past complaints. Quintilian
(circa 100) observed that, just as cities can bring together and exacerbate
the problem of social undesirables, so too Moses knit together scattered
individuals into a single Jewish tribe: "founders of cities are detested
[when] concentrating a race which is a curse (*perniciosam*—i.e. pernicious) to others, as for example the founder of the Jewish superstition".[9]
Damocritus' book *Peri Ioudaion* (On the Jews) argued that "they used to
worship an asinine golden head, and that every seventh year they caught
a foreigner and sacrificed him"[10]—in contrast to the story by Posidonius
in which the sacrifice was an annual event.

---

[8] In Stern (1974: 444).
[9] In Stern (1974: 513).
[10] In Stern (1974: 531).

One new criticism came from the writings of Roman poet Martial (aka Marcus Martialis). In the fourth book of his *Epigrams,* he undertakes to lambast an acquaintance of his, named Bassa, by calling attention to his evidently horrible body odor. To drive the point home, Martial compares Bassa's smell to a host of notoriously pungent things: the odor of a drained marsh, the "sulphurous waters of Albula," "the putrid stench of a marine fish-pond," someone's old shoes, and… "the breath of the fasting Jews" (*quod ieiunia sabbatariarum*).[11] It is widely known, even today, that fasting can produce or exacerbate bad breath, and the ancient Jews were infamous for fasting on the Sabbath day; hence the correlation is perfectly understandable. Still, Martial's point comes through quite clearly: Jewish breath was a benchmark of foul smell. More importantly, Martial established the historical precedent for the so-called *foetor Judaicus*—the "Jewish stench" critique that would recur at various times throughout history, notably with Schopenhauer.

The renowned writer and philosopher Plutarch made several comments on Jews, mostly neutral observations but occasionally interspersed with statements about their "superstitions" and odd habit of keeping the Sabbath. His dialogue *Morals* (IV, 4) includes an examination of the nature of the Jewish God, and of the question "Whether the Jews abstain from pork because of reverence or aversion for the pig." (He concludes that they worship the pig, in addition to the ass.)

*****

This brings us to Tacitus—one of the great historians of the ancient world, and one of the most notable critics of the tribe from Judea. His chief work, *Histories*, is an invaluable historical study, but let me first cite an observation from his other main book, *Annals* (circa 115 AD). Amidst an examination of the great fire of Rome that had occurred back in the year 64, Tacitus comments on the Jews and that new Jewish cult, Christianity:

> Nero…punished with the utmost refinements…a class of
> men, loathed for their vices, whom the crowd styled Chris-

---

[11] Martial (1897).

tians (*Chrestianos*). Christus, the founder of the name, had undergone the death penalty in the reign of Tiberius, by sentence of the procurator Pontius Pilate, and the pernicious superstition was checked for a moment, only to break out once more—not merely in Judaea, the home of the disease, but in the capital [Rome] itself, where all things horrible or shameful in the world collect and find a vogue. (XV, 44)[12]

The Jews, he continues, were persecuted not so much for involvement with the fire as simply because of their misanthropy, their "hatred of the human race" (*odio humani generis*)—a phrase that was destined to be recalled throughout history. So severe was Nero that, in some cases, Jews "were burned to serve as lamps by night." Tacitus' comments clearly indicate the low status of the Jews: loathsome, vice-ridden, pernicious, superstitious…even, ominously, a "disease"—a striking biological metaphor that recalls Claudius. The reference to 'Christus' is significant; it predates Suetonius' comment by some 20 years, and marks the earliest Roman acknowledgment of the founder of the new religion.

But it is the *Histories*—written about the year 100—that contains an extended critique of the Jews.[13] In Book V, Tacitus recounts historical events from the year 70 AD. Roman general Titus had been sent to subjugate Judea once and for all. He found allies in the indigenous Arabs, "who hated the Jews with all that hatred that is common among neighbors" (5.1)—hence proving that the enmities of that region are truly deep-seated.

Tacitus then breaks off the narrative to give an account of the origin of the Jews—that "race of men hateful to the gods" (*genus hominum invisium deis*). He offers two or three variations, apparently siding with Manetho. The religion of Moses, he adds, is diametrically opposed to that of the Romans: "The Jews regard as profane all that we hold sacred; on the other hand, they permit all that we abhor." He continues:

Whatever their origin, these rites are maintained by their antiquity: the other customs of the Jews are base and abom-

---

[12] In Stern (1980: 89). See also Tacitus, *Annals* (2012), p. 325.
[13] See Tacitus, *The Histories* (1997), pp. 233-236.

inable (*sinistra foeda*), and owe their persistence to their depravity. For the worst rascals among other peoples…always kept sending tribute and contributions to Jerusalem, thereby increasing the wealth of the Jews; again, the Jews are extremely loyal toward one another, and always ready to show compassion, but toward every other people they feel only hate and enmity (*hostile odium*).

"As a race," he adds, "they are prone to lust," and have "adopted circumcision to distinguish themselves from other peoples" (5.5). Tacitus notes their abstract monotheism, suggesting that this is yet another cause of friction. He closes the section with the comment that "the ways of the Jews are preposterous (*absurdus*) and mean (*sordidus*)."

In besieging Jerusalem, and later the mighty Jewish temple, Titus had the Jews trapped, explains Tactitus. There was thought of sparing the temple, but the Romans opposed this option. For Titus, "the destruction of this temple [was] a prime necessity in order to wipe out (*tolleretur*) more completely the religion of the Jews and the Christians." These two religions, "although hostile to each other, nevertheless sprang from the same sources; the Christians had grown out of the Jews: if the root were destroyed, the stock would easily perish" (*Fragments of the Histories*). The passage closes by noting that 600,000 Jews were killed in the war.

Such are Tacitus' comments on the "obnoxious and superstitious race" (*gens superstitioni obnoxia*; 5.13)—a group who are the "most despised" (*despectissima*) of subjects and "the basest of peoples" (*taeterrimam gentum*; 5.8). Both because of his clear articulation and his general authority, Tacitus is the single most-cited ancient authority regarding criticism of the Jews. Many later scholars, including Gibbon, Schopenhauer, and Nietzsche, quote him on the topic.

Present-day Jewish authors, on the other hand, are hard-pressed to account for such a negative assessment; it would be a real challenge, for example, to portray Tacitus as mentally ill. Most often one finds an attempt to whitewash the whole affair, ascribing Tacitus' remarks to 'the spirit of the times,' or as merely reactionary. Erich Gruen (2011) is typical; he spends several pages arguing that Tacitus wasn't portraying his own *personal* opinion, but rather simply making a sarcastic social commentary in order to "tease" and "challenge" the reader. The *Histories* give us not the historian's own view, says Gruen, but "a sardonic comment on simplistic stereotypes." Tacitus omits the "far harsher assessments" of Manetho and Apion, and "does not deliver his own judgment." In sum, "we hear the voice of the sardonic historian, not the Jew hater" (2011: 190, 192). Unlikely, to say the least.

The second Jewish revolt, in 115, gave further cause for critique. Cassius Dio describes the action graphically in his *Roman History*:

> Meanwhile the Jews in the region of Cyrene had put a certain Andreas at their head, and were destroying both the Romans and the Greeks. They would eat the flesh of their victims, make belts for themselves of their entrails, anoint themselves with their blood, and wear their skins for clothing; many they sawed in two, from the head downwards; others they gave to wild beasts, and still others they forced to fight as gladiators. (Book 68.32)

Here we have the Philo problem, in reverse: Should we believe Dio's extreme statements about the viciousness of the Jews, or is he exaggerating? We have no directly comparable account, but it is roughly consistent with both Manetho's and Lysimachus' Exodus stories and accompanying Jewish brutalities. The question remains open.

But it was perhaps such incidences that prompted Juvenal and Suetonius to comment. In his famous *Satires*, Juvenal (ca. 120) makes at least three references to Jews. The first is a jab at the allegedly incestuous relationship between the Jewish king Agrippa II and his sister Berenice, rulers of "that barbarian country…where pigs are free to live to a ripe old age" (6.153-160). Later he remarks on a poor Jewess fortune-teller, begging for coins:

> This High Priestess has to live under a tree, but she knows all the secrets of Heaven. She, too, will fill her palm, but not too full: a few coppers purchase, where Jews are concerned, fulfillment of dreams and fancies. (6.542-547)

Finally, in the 14th satire, Juvenal ridicules the Jews' customs of circumcision, worshipping a 'sky god,' avoiding pork, keeping the Sabbath, and the generally adverse effects on their children (14.96-106):

> Those whose lot it was that their fathers worshipped the Sabbath
> Pray to nothing now but the clouds and a spirit in Heaven;
> Since their fathers abstained from pork, they'd be cannibals sooner
> Than violate that taboo. Circumcised, not as the Gentiles,
> They despise Roman law, but learn and observe and revere
> Israel's code, and all from the sacred volume of Moses
> Where the way is not shown to any but true believers,
> Where the uncircumcised are never led to the fountain.
> *Remember the Sabbath Day, to keep it lazy.* The father,
> Setting this day apart from life, is the cause and culprit.

Suetonius, writing about the reign of Domitian (81-96 AD), makes a passing comment on the 'Jew tax' (*Iudaicus fiscus*) that was levied after the destruction of the temple in 70 AD. "Besides other taxes, that on the Jews was levied with the utmost vigor…".[14] Many Jews attempted to hide their race simply to avoid the tax, and it was sometimes necessary, he says, to strip men naked and check for circumcision as proof. This tax continued well into the 200s.

The third and final Jewish uprising occurred just a few years later, in 132. The reasons for this were many, but two stand out: the construction of a Roman city on the ruins of Jerusalem, and emperor Hadrian's banning of circumcision: "At this time the Jews began war, because they were forbidden to practice genital mutilation (*mutilare genitalia*)".[15]

Dio describes the conflict in detail. "Jews everywhere were showing signs of hostility to the Romans, partly by secret and partly overt acts" (*Roman History* 69.13). They were able to bribe others to join in the uprising: "many outside nations, too, were joining them through eagerness for gain, and the whole earth, one might almost say, was being stirred up over the matter." For those today who argue that Jews were perennially the cause of wars, this would provide some early evidence. Hadrian sent

---

[14] In Stern (1980: 128). See also Suetonius, *The Twelve Caesars* (1979), p. 308.
[15] *Historiae Augustae*, 14. In Stern (1980: 619).

one of his best generals, Severus, to put down the insurgency. Through a slow war of attrition, "he was able...to crush, exhaust, and exterminate (*ekkophai*) them. Very few of them in fact survived." Mary Boatwright estimates that 580,000 Jews were killed.[16]

To close this section, I will look at two final figures of the second century. Famed astronomer Ptolemy was also a bit of an astrologer, and took to using the stars to explain earthly conditions. In his *Apotelesmatica* of 150 AD, Ptolemy observes that the tribes of Palestine, including Idumaea, Syria, Judea, and Phoenicia, have some common characteristics.

> These people...are more gifted in trade and exchange; they are more unscrupulous, despicable cowards, treacherous, servile, and in general fickle, on account of the stars mentioned. [The Judaeans in particular] are in general bold, godless, and scheming. (II, 3)[17]

'Born under a bad sign,' as they say. Given the four centuries of conflict with the people of that region, Ptolemy can hardly be blamed for viewing them as cursed by the heavens.

Finally we have Celsus, a Greek philosopher who composed a text, *The True Word*, sometime around 178. The piece is striking as an extended and scathing critique of the newly-emerging Christian sect.[18] It survives only as extended quotations in Origen's book of the year 248, *Contra Celsum.*

Celsus' target is clearly Christianity, but in the process, he makes a number of remarks on the Jews—all negative. Beginning with Moses, the Jews "were deluded by clumsy deceits into thinking that there was

---

[16] Boatwright (2008) is mystified that, even after all their difficulties, the Romans were still generally tolerant of other religions, including the radical Christians—all religions except, apparently, the Jews. "It is hard to reconcile Hadrian's insensitivity toward the Jews with the ample evidence for his open support of many different rituals and shrines" (p. 174)—hard only if one does not understand the history and context.

[17] In Stern (1980: 165).

[18] It was written very much in the style of Lorenzo Valla's "Discourse on the Forgery of the Alleged Donation of Constantine" of 1440. One can surmise that Valla took it as his inspiration.

only one God" (I.23). They were "addicted to sorcery" and thus "fell into error through ignorance and were deceived." Celsus mocks "the race of Jews and Christians," comparing them all "to a cluster of bats or ants coming out of a nest, or frogs holding council round a marsh, or worms assembling in some filthy corner, disagreeing with each other about which of them are the worse sinners" (IV.23). (More biological imagery.) "The Jews," he adds, "were runaway slaves who escaped from Egypt; they never did anything important, nor have they ever been of any significance or prominence" (IV.31). Fate has been justifiably harsh to them, and they are "suffering the penalty of their arrogance" (V.41).

Judeo-Christian theology, says Celsus, is a mish-mash of mythology and absurdity. "The God of the Jews is accursed" because he created, or allowed, evil in the world—a classic statement of the Problem of Evil. The cosmogony of Genesis is ridiculous, as is the creation story of mankind; "Moses wrote these stories because he understood nothing… [He] put together utter trash" (VI.49). In the long run Jewry is doomed—"they will presently perish" (VI.80).

An Empire Declines, a Religion Ascends

Events turned sour for Rome during the 200s. Imperial expansion had peaked by 120 AD, and the Goths and Persians mounted increasingly successful attacks. Roman leadership became harsher and more authoritarian; suppression of foreign religions and cults increased, with particular focus on Christianity.

Dio's *Roman History*, dating to 220, made a notably grim assessment of things. Above I quoted his passages relating to the revolts in 115 and 132, but he makes a few other relevant comments. Book 37 relates the initial capture of Jerusalem by Pompey, and thus the first direct encounter with the Jews. "They are distinguished from the rest of mankind in practically every detail of life." One must proceed carefully, Dio suggests, "for the race is very bitter when aroused to anger" (49.22). Near the end of the work he mentions the 'Jew tax'—"an annual tribute of two *denarii*" (65.7)—that we saw in the fragment from Suetonius.

Ten years later, the Greek sophist and writer Philostratus produced a biography of the philosopher Apollonius of Tyana, who lived a century earlier. In the midst of a passage attacking the cruelty of Nero, Philostratus remarks on the Roman military's penchant for battling Jews rather than dealing with problems at home:

> The Jews have long been in revolt not only against the Romans, but against all humanity (*panton anthropon*); and a race that has made its own a life apart and irreconcilable, that cannot share with the rest of mankind in the pleasures of the table nor join in their libations or prayers or sacrifices, are separated from ourselves by a greater gulf than divides us from Susa or Bactra or the more distant Indies. (V.33.4)

Dio and Philostratus are raising the stakes: Not only are the Jews enemies of humanity, they are profoundly *different* than the rest—separated by a vast gulf, different in every detail. Philostratus obviously had no understanding of genetics, but he certainly indicates that Jews are somehow biologically different, and worse, than ordinary men.

The persistence of the charge of misanthropy is remarkable. It appears yet again in a work by Neoplatonist philosopher Porphyry, in his work *Adversus Christianos* (Against the Christians), circa 280. Writing a tract comparable to that of Celsus, Porphyry also draws in the Jews. He comments on the "foreign mythologies" of the Jews (I, 2), seen as "evil report among all men." The Jews, he adds, are "the impious enemies of all nations".[19]

Justinus—also known as Justin the Historian—composed his lengthy *Historiarum Philippicarum* in the year 300. Book 36 addresses the origin of the Jews. He reiterates the leprosy exodus story of Manetho: The Egyptians, "being troubled with scabies and leprosy…expelled [Moses], with those who had the disease, out of Egypt." In an interesting and benign twist, the Jews, being concerned about spreading their disease, voluntarily adopt a policy of disengagement:

> And as they remembered that they had been driven from Egypt for fear of spreading infection, they took care, in order

---

[19] The same quotation was cited a few decades later by the Christian historian Eusebius, in his *Preparation for the Gospel* (I.2).

that they might not become odious, from the same cause, to the inhabitants of the country, to have no communication with strangers; a rule which, from having been adopted on that particular occasion, gradually became a custom and part of their religion. (36.2)

After establishing themselves in Judea, they created a form of theocracy that merged religion with politics. This gave them a cohesiveness and unity of purpose that proved highly successful. As a result, "it is almost incredible how powerful they became."

CHAPTER 3
TRANSITION TO A CHRISTIAN WORLDVIEW

I have been a stranger in a strange land.
—Exodus 2:22

For Christians, Jews were eternal strangers.
—J. Hood (1995: 22)

After 300 AD, the Empire went into steady decline and Christianity began to assert its power. Emperor Constantine converted in 312, giving the young religion official endorsement. In 380, Emperor Theodosius I effectively made it the state religion. By this time, there was a relatively clear distinction between the Gentile Christian church and the orthodox Judaic Jews. As a result of this, and due to the 'family feud' involved with Christianity arising from Judaism and the Jews having 'killed Christ,' conditions for the Hebrew tribe worsened.

A series of imperial legislative actions between 329 and 438 specifically targeted the Jews, and we have detailed records of many of these:

- Constantine's edict of 18 October 329 bars the Jews from punishing anyone choosing to "escape from their deadly sect." Conversely, anyone electing to join "their nefarious sect" will be punished.

- His successor, Constantine II, warned against Jews who proselytized women "in depravity" (*turpitudinis*).

- On 21 May 383, Gratian warns that those who have "polluted themselves with the Jewish contagions" (*Iudaicis semet polluere contagiis*) will be punished.

- Honorius decreed, on 1 April 409, that none shall "adopt the abominable and vile name of the Jews"; no one must accept "the Jewish perversity (*perversitatem*), which is alien to the Roman Empire."

- On 31 January 438, Theodosius II referred to "the blindly sense-
  less Jews," calling them "monstrous heretics" and an "abominable sect," and declared that "no Jew…should accede to honors
  and dignities".[1]

All was not hopeless for them, however. A joint edict of 6 August 420
stated that "No one shall be destroyed for being a Jew".[2] But it adds a
warning, "lest the Jews grow perchance insolent, and elated by their security, commit something rash against the reverence of the Christian cult
(*cultionis*)."

Emperor Julian (reign 355-363) was an interesting and complex
character. Rather like Aurelius, he was both a great military commander
and a notable writer and philosopher. Christianity had been increasingly
accepted within the Empire since 310, but Julian strongly opposed it,
much preferring the values and beliefs of the original Roman republic.
Thus he sought to mitigate the growing power of the Christians. One way
to do this was to elevate the status of their chief rival, Judaism. Julian
thereby became a 'friend of the Jews,' though only insofar as they served
his larger purposes. In reality, he had a profound dislike of the entire
Judeo-Christian worldview.

This aspect of his thinking appears in his essay *Contra Galilaeus*
(Against the Galileans), circa 361. He criticizes those who would leave
Christianity for Judaism as a kind of leap from the frying pan into the
fire—something no reasonable person would do. "The philosophers," he
says, "bid us to imitate the gods so far as we can. … But what sort of
imitation of God is praised among the Hebrews? Anger and wrath and
fierce jealousy" (171d-e). God evidently does not favor the Jews, because "he bestowed on the Hebrews nothing considerable or of great value" (176a). They indeed imitate the cruelty of their god: "the most wick-
ed and most brutal of the [Roman] generals behaved more mildly to the
greatest offenders than Moses did to those who had done no wrong"
(184c). They who abandon Roman ways "emulate the rages and the bit-
terness of the Jews." The Jewish race has given rise to no great leaders,
generals, intellectuals, artists, nor even a civilized society; government,

---

[1] In Linder (1987), pages 126-127, 148, 171, 258, and 329, respectively.
[2] In Linder, p. 285.

law courts, laws, liberal arts... "were not all these things in a miserable and barbarous state among the Hebrews?" (221e). In the end, of course, Julian failed to either raise up the Jews or to halt the slide toward Christianity. He died in battle in the year 363, at only 32 years of age, and thus was unable to complete his project of reform.

Julian's close confidant, Ammianus Marcellinus, was also one of the last great Roman historians of ancient times. In his *History*, Ammianus recounts the journey of Emperor Marcus Aurelius (reigned 161 to 180 AD) through the Middle East, whereupon he encountered the Jews; apparently it was not a pleasant experience:

> For Marcus, as he was passing through Palestine on his way to Egypt, being often disgusted with the malodorous (*fetentium*) and rebellious Jews, is reported to have cried with sorrow: "O Marcomanni, O Quadi, O Sarmatians, at last I have found a people more unruly than you".[3]

As usual, the veracity of this report is questionable, as we have no confirming statements. But even if this was Ammianus' own view, it is noteworthy. The reference to "malodorous Jews" recalls Martial; and in fact, both of these sources would be repeatedly cited in later centuries.

Into the 400s, we find the work of prominent Roman poet Rutilius Namatianus. His lone surviving piece, *De Reditu Suo*, casts light on many aspects of the late period of the Empire. Rutilius relates a story of how he was pausing to rest beside a pond one day, on land that turned out to be owned by a Jew. In typical form, the Jew demands a fee for the use of his land (I, 385-398):[4]

> We pay the abuse due to the filthy race
> that famously practices circumcision;
> a root of silliness they are:
> chill Sabbaths are after their own heart,
> yet their heart is chillier than their creed.
> Each seventh day is condemned to ignoble sloth,

---

[3] In Stern (1980: 606).
[4] In Stern (1980: 663). See also Joyce (2021) for an extended discussion.

as 'twere an effeminate picture of the god fatigued.
The other wild ravings from their lying bazaar methinks
not even a child in his sleep could believe.
And would that Judea had never been subdued
by Pompey's wars and Titus' military power!
The infection of this plague, though excised, still creeps
    abroad the more:
and 'tis their own conquerors that a conquered race keeps
    down.

Again we find the biological metaphors, harsher than ever. The "infection of this plague" (*pestis contagia*) suggests once more the need for disinfection, if not outright extermination.

In any case, Rome's time was over. The Empire fractured into two realms in 395, just 15 years after Theodosius made Christianity the state religion. The classical (western) half would survive another 80 years, until its final collapse in 476. The popes and the church filled the void, shepherding Europe through the Dark Ages. Antagonism toward the Jews took a decidedly theological turn, which combined with preexisting cultural, moral, and racial antipathies to produce a complex and fascinating anti-Jewish worldview.

Thus it is clear, and indisputable, that the vast majority of ancient remarks on the Jews were negative. This is not a consequence of mere 'cherry-picking' of critical comments but rather a reflection of the reality of the situation—a reality acknowledged by most scholars in the field. Margaret Williams (1998: 161) indirectly reinforces this point in her discussion of a passage from Strabo, which is "one of the few favorable treatments of Judaism to survive from Graeco-Roman antiquity." Anti-Jewish attitudes were widespread and persistent in the ancient world. This is not a coincidence, and it's not just bad luck. There is clearly something endemic to the Jewish people that elicits such remarks.[5]

An analysis of these comments finds a number of enduring themes that form the basis for this generally anti-Jewish stance. In summary, these reasons include: a crude fixation on money and material wealth;

---

[5] There has been one notable attempt to document pro-Jewish commentary from ancient times; I address this in chapter 10.

human sacrifice (or "blood libel"[6]); misanthropy; cursed by the gods; cowardly and reckless; failure to contribute to civilization; superstitious; disproportionately powerful; 'pushy'; malodorous; marked by genital mutilation (circumcision); lazy (no work on the Sabbath); seditious; vice-ridden; and, generally speaking, a plague on humanity.

To emphasize, these were not mindless expressions of rage or brute anti-Semitism. These were objective and well-considered observations by the brightest men of the age, commenting on a set of real and non-trivial social problems. Rome was a tolerant and inclusive society; the writers were educated and open-minded individuals, with no evident pre-disposition to be anti-Jewish. This was simply their experience based on centuries of interaction with the tribe from Judea.

Such complaints form the historical basis for an enduring and deeply-rooted anti-Jewish attitude that can be found throughout much of the world, and throughout much of history. Many of these themes recur to the present day, and their origins and evolution reveal important aspects of modern-day Jews. More broadly, we can infer that the critics are citing objective, concrete characteristics of the Jewish people, ones that are largely independent of Judaism per se. These negative qualities seem rooted in the genetic (i.e. racial) constitution of the Jews, and this suggests an explanation for their persistence across cultures and over time.

Early Middle Ages and the Rise of the Church

The Western Roman Empire entered its final years in the 5th century AD. The Church was ascendant, and would soon begin a thousand-year domination of European culture. Christianity from its start was in tension with the Jewish community, as we know from the story of Jesus and his disciples. All the early Christians were Jews, but they were in revolt against both the elite (Jewish) Pharisees and the dominant Roman Empire. Jesus and his followers made enemies on both fronts, and both were complicit in his death.

But even if we are inclined to disbelieve the traditional story of Christ—and there is good reason to doubt it—we still have his disciples

---

[6] For a recent study on Jewish blood libel and human sacrifice in the Renaissance, see Toaff (2020).

to deal with. On some interpretations, Paul, along with Luke, Mark, and Peter, deliberately undertook to challenge the Romans by creating an alternate moral system and, in fact, a completely new worldview—one that involved a savior come to Earth. This action put the small band of rebels in conflict with an age-old Jewish tradition that was still awaiting its savior. To have any hope of undermining support for Rome, the newly-minted Christian story had to draw in as many gentiles as possible. Christianity thus, at the very start, pitted (lowly) Jew against (elite) Jew and all against Rome. As the movement expanded beyond its Jewish origins, and Rome disintegrated, the central conflict to remain was Christian against Jew.

But again, in the early years, both Jews and non-Jewish Christians were allied against Rome, and they had little reason to disagree. Thus it was that, at this time, we find only mild criticism of the Jews—two examples being Tertullian's *Adversus Judaeos* and Hippolytus' *Expository Treatise against the Jews*, both written circa 200. These offer only the faintest rebukes, and serve primarily to distinguish the nascent Christians from their Jewish roots. But then Emperor Constantine converted in 315, and by 380 Theodosius had declared Christianity as the state religion; the Empire would then disintegrate within a few decades. That final Christian century of the Empire saw the rise of much stronger anti-Jewish sentiments, as it became clear that the two sibling religions would be vying for control.

Four of the most important early church fathers—Gregory of Nyssa, Jerome of Stridon, John Chrysostom, and Augustine—were notably anti-Jewish. Writing in the late 300s, Gregory blasts the Jews as the absolute dregs of humanity, deploying an impressive array of adjectives:

> Murderers of the Lord, murderers of prophets, rebels and full of hatred against God, they commit outrage against the law, resist God's grace, repudiate the faith of their fathers. They are confederates of the devil, offspring of vipers, scandal-mongers, slanderers, darkened in mind, leaven of the Pharisees, Sanhedrin of demons, accursed, utterly vile,

> quick to abuse, enemies of all that is good. (*In Christi res-urr. orat.*, 5).[7]

Clearly there is more here than a religious family feud; Gregory evidently finds something deeply objectionable in the Jews themselves.

Similar thoughts are portrayed in the writings of Jerome (347-420), a Christian abbot in Bethlehem. Jaher (1994: 30) suggests that Jerome "anticipated modern anti-Semitism propaganda by predicting the emergence of an infernal Jewish conspiracy for global domination." In 407 Jerome wrote that the antichrist would be "born of the Jewish people"; "by means of intrigue and deception," the Jews would "persecute the people of Christ [and] rule the world." Of course, it turned out that this was not merely "propaganda" but a strikingly accurate prediction, albeit one that would take some 1500 years to materialize.

Speaking of the synagogue, Jerome wrote, "If you call it a brothel, a den of vice, the Devil's refuge, Satan's fortress, a place to deprave the soul…you are still saying less than it deserves".[8] Hood (1995: 16) adds that he "accused the Jews of almost every imaginable vice, but avarice, drunkenness, gluttony, and licentiousness were his favorites." Living as he did directly amongst them, Jerome undoubtedly had considerable firsthand experience.

Of all the early church fathers, though, Chrysostom is widely viewed as the most openly hostile. Of particular note is his work *Adversus Judaeos*, commonly called *Homilies Against the Jews* (387 AD).[9] The first homily captures the essence of his attack. He begins with mention of a "very serious illness" that pervades society. "What is this disease? The festivals of the pitiful and miserable Jews" which were soon to commence (I.I.5; p. 4). "But do not be surprised that I call the Jews pitiable," he adds. "They really are pitiable and miserable" (I.II.1; p. 5). Citing Biblical precedent, Chrysostom refers to them as dogs, and as "stiff-necked." They are drawn to gluttony and drunkenness (I.II.5; p. 7), and chiefly characterized by their lust for animal pleasures. Indeed, they are animals, though of a worthless kind: "Although such beasts are unfit for

---

[7] In Simon (1996: 216).
[8] In Wistrich (2010: 80).
[9] Also known as *Discourses Against the Jews*. The following quotations are taken from the new (2025) edition, published by Clemens & Blair.

work, they are fit for killing" (I.II.6; p. 7)—a shocking call from this man of God. "And this is what happened to the Jews: while they were making themselves unfit for work, they grew fit for slaughter." He even cites Biblical mandate here, from the Gospel of Luke (19:27): "This is why Christ said, 'But as for these my enemies, ...bring them here and slay them'."

Chrysostom disparages the religious rituals of the synagogue: "[The Jews] drag into the synagogue the whole theater, actors and all. For there is no difference between the theater and the synagogue" (I.II.7). "That place is a brothel," he adds. "It is also a den of robbers and a lodging for wild beasts." In fact it has become no less than "the dwelling of demons" (I.III.1; p. 8)—as "the Jews themselves are demons" (I.VI.3; p. 16).

He then raises a fundamental metaphysical dispute. The Christian testament speaks of a bifurcated afterlife: either eternal bliss with God in heaven, or eternal damnation. "But the Jews," says Chrysostom,

> neither know nor dream of these things.[10] They live for their bellies, they gape for the things of this world, their condition is no better than that of pigs or goats because of their wanton ways and excessive gluttony. They know but one thing: to fill their bellies and be drunk... (I.IV.1; p. 10)

Then there are the standard charges of the Jews as Christ-killers, and as failing to properly honor the old prophets: "And so it is that we must hate both them and their synagogue all the more because of the offensive treatment of those holy men." On a more practical level, the Jews are to be shunned because of "their plundering, their covetousness, their abandonment of the poor, their thefts, their cheating in trade" (I.VII.1; p. 17)—charges that relate to fundamental cultural and ethnic traits, rather than religion.

And once again we find reference to the bad smell—the *foetor Judaicus*—that seems to accompany the Jews. This time, though, it comes from the alleged sacrificial burning of human victims that attends the synagogue festival, and the potent incense used to cover it up:

---

[10] In truth, the Old Testament has virtually no mention of either an afterlife with God in heaven, or, astonishingly, of hell. For the Jews, all praise or retribution occurs in the present world. This fact likely explains much of the traditional Jewish obsession with material goods, money, wealth, and power.

> Yet what is carried up from the altar is the odor and smoke from burning bodies, and nothing is more malodorous than such a savor. … Scripture calls…the incense an abomination because the intention of those offering it reeked with a great stench (I.VII.3; p. 18).

For all these reasons, says Chrysostom, we must "turn away from them, since they are the common disgrace and infection of the whole world" (I.VI.7)—recalling Claudius' imagery of a "general plague that infests the whole world." Finally, Chrysostom appeals to his Christian reader to not fear the Jews' sorcery and black powers; "the Jews frighten you as if you were little children, and you do not see it" (I.III.7). Such a sentiment could be repeated in the present day, as many gentiles seem to act in evident fear of hidden Jewish power of retribution, as if afraid of some evil spell; it was disgraceful then and it is disgraceful now.

We lack direct evidence, but such forceful talk by prominent church leaders no doubt encouraged discrimination and violence against the Jews, and likely contributed, for example, to their expulsion from Alexandria in the year 414.

Augustine is the most famous and influential of this early group, and he is also the most understated in his criticism. On the one hand, he views the Jews as "incurably 'carnal,' blind to spiritual meaning, perfidious, faithless, and apostate".[11] In his *Adversus Judaeos*, circa 425, he denounces them for ignoring the revealed truth about God—an especially pernicious crime, since it was handed to them and yet they refused it. Consequently, "they are themselves the builders of destruction and rejecters of the corner-stone".[12] John Cavadini (1999: 13) explains that, in the *Adversus*, Augustine adopts "a more negative image" of the Jews than in his other writings, casting upon them sole blame for the crucifixion ("It was the Jews who held [Jesus]; the Jews who insulted him; the Jews who bound him; the Jews who crowned him with thorns; who soiled him with their spit; who whipped him; who ridiculed him; who hung him on the cross; who stabbed his body with their spears").[13] Augustine fur-

---

[11] Wistrich (2010: 86).
[12] In Carroll (2001: 215).
[13] In Michael (2008: 17).

thermore links them with many ignoble characteristics; they are "blind, stubborn, sick," and lacking in understanding.

On the other hand, the Jews are 'living witnesses' to the truth of the Christian story, and thus ought to be preserved, not destroyed, because they serve as enduring testimony. This is made clear in Augustine's *City of God*:

> [T]he Jews who killed [Christ] refused to believe in him... They were dispersed all over the world—for indeed there is no part of the earth where they are not to be found—and thus by evidence of their own Scriptures they bear witness for us that we have not fabricated the prophecies about Christ. ... [T]hey supply for our benefit by the possession and preservation of those books... [Were they not scattered, we] would not have them available among all nations as witnesses to the prophecies which were given beforehand concerning Christ. (Book 18)

Augustine thus introduces a tension into Christian-Jewish relations that endures today: the Jews are ignorant and blind, yet confirm the truth of the Bible; they must be preserved as living relics, but not allowed to hold sway over society or the minds of men. This sense of "destructive ambivalence"[14] would both justify and forestall violence against the Jews for centuries.

Toward the Renaissance: From Agobard to Erasmus

With the final collapse of Rome in 476 and the onset of the early Middle Ages (the so-called Dark Ages), the Church began a long, gradual climb toward dominance of European culture and society. Jews remained on the periphery—though never far from the seat of power. Charlemagne (circa 800) treated them with a kind of political expediency, allowing a modest degree of freedom in business and commerce but restricting their abilities to proselytize. Charlemagne's son, Louis the Pious (778-840), was notably friendly toward the Jews, enacting a charter of privilege for

---

[14] Carroll (2001: 219).

them. Evidently he was of the view that he would personally profit from a Jewish alliance. Jews of the realm were, at that time, "militant, aggressive, and powerful",[15] and were heavily involved in the growing slave trade of Europe. This fact, combined with their imperial charter, meant that Jews were in more a superior social position even than the Christians.

This situation drew the attention of archbishop Agobard of Lyon, who complained to Louis in a letter of 826 titled "On the insolence of the Jews." The Jews, he writes, "set up a persecuting faction against the Church," targeted at Agobard himself. Furthermore, "the Jews daily curse Jesus Christ and the Christians," engage in slave trading of Christians, and pass off their unclean meats to the unsuspecting Gentile public. In sum, the Jews are "detestable enemies of the truth".[16]

As the second millennium AD began, Christianity faced increasing pressure from, and confrontation with, both Jews and Muslims. The Caliphate of Cordoba ruled much of the Iberian Peninsula, where Muslims dominated since taking hold there in the 700s; prominent Jewish communities existed not only in Iberia but throughout much of Italy and across southern France, and their influence was pressing north rapidly. One Christian to object to this Jewish incursion was Peter the Venerable (1092-1156), whose work *Against the Inveterate Obduracy of the Jews* (circa 1145) was a milestone in Christian criticism. More extensive even than Chrysostom's *Homilies*, it was the first to specifically attack the Talmud as a source of error and mischief for Jews.[17]

By the time of the Fourth Lateran Council of 1215, Pope Innocent III was prepared to reassert control. New resolutions (canons) were passed, "designed to isolate, restrict, and denigrate Jews".[18] Usury was a growing problem, especially when it was causing the bankruptcy of church members who were expected to donate generously. Canon 67 reads: "The more the Christians are restrained from the practice of usury, the more are they oppressed in this matter by the treachery of the Jews,

---

[15] Bachrach (1977: 104).

[16] For the full letter, see Volume Two of *Classic Essays on the Jewish Question* (2025). Agobard's successor, Amulo of Lyons, also wrote against the Jews; his letter to King Charles, dated 845 AD, begins: "How abominably crafty these Jews are!"

[17] For more on Peter, see Chazan (2016), pp. 120-131.

[18] Carroll (2001: 282).

so that in a short time they exhaust the resources of the Christians." There was also the problem of identification. Then as now, Jews were largely able to move unnoticed through gentile society, owing to the lack of obvious ethnic features. This was unacceptable to the Church and hence they mandated a "difference of dress" for Jews (and also Muslims, or "Saracens"): "we decree that such Jews and Saracens of both sexes in every Christian province and at all times shall be marked off in the eyes of the public from other peoples through the character of their dress" (Canon 68). This was no idle declaration; conical caps, badges, and related clothing were instituted in France, Portugal, Spain, and Italy in the following centuries.[19] Finally, Canon 69 states that "Jews are not to be given public offices… [because] it is absurd that a blasphemer of Christ exercise authority over Christians."

This harsher stance was taken up by the preeminent theologian of the day, Thomas Aquinas. In contrast to Augustine, Aquinas preferred to emphasize the fact that the Jews knowingly sinned in first refusing and then crucifying the Savior. As Hood (1995: 74) writes, "In Aquinas' view, the Jewish leaders had sufficient evidence to know that Jesus was divine, but they willfully refused to draw the conclusion. This increased rather than limited their culpability." This guilt, Aquinas says, is furthermore perpetually binding on the Jewish people, so long as they refuse Christ and adhere to Mosaic Law: "The blood of Christ binds the children of the Jews insofar as they are imitators of their parents' malice and thus approve of Christ's killing" (*Questiones Disputata de Malo*, 4.8).

Apart from this theological guilt was the practical problem of usury. Normally defined as lending money at excessive interest, for Aquinas usury meant *any* interest. As he writes in the *Summa Theologica*, "Lending money at interest is intrinsically unjust" (ST_{2-2}, 78.1). All interest is unethical because it entails no effort; it is reward without work, hardly better than sheer theft. That this is a crime is manifestly obvious to Aquinas, and thus calls for the harshest of punishment. And the Jews come in for special reprimand, as they were most closely identified with that crime. "It seems to me that a Jew, or any other usurer, should be fined more heavily than others who are punished with fines, since they are known to have less title to the money taken from them" (*De Regimine*

---

[19] See Jaher (1994: 70).

Judaeorum [On the Government of the Jews], 70-74). Monarchs of Europe would suffer from restrictions on interest, but they have an obligation to rein in the usurers: "It would be better for [royalty] to compel Jews to work for a living, as is done in parts of Italy, than to allow them to live in idleness and grow rich by usury. If rulers suffer loss, it is only because they have been negligent" (*De Regimine*, 81-88).[20]

The Jews were guilty on both philosophical and pragmatic counts, and thus were to be shunned. For Aquinas, "Jews were profoundly dangerous, and…contact with them should be avoided whenever possible".[21] One should not socialize or eat with them, discuss religion, or marry them; they were indeed the true "enemies" of Christian society (ST$_{2-2}$, 10.11). Aquinas upheld the Lateran Council's dictate on restricting Jews from public office, and he endorsed the call to mark them with distinctive clothing. On this latter point he wrote, "The response to this question is clear, since, according to the statue of the general [Lateran] council, Jews of each sex in all Christian lands and at all times should be distinguished from other people by their dress" (*De Regimine*, 244-249). The point is obvious but it bears repeating: the act of identifying one's enemy is the first step in dealing with him.

For theological, sociological, and practical reasons, then, the nations of Europe began to take action by banishing their Jewish populations. England was among the first to act: King Edward I expelled all Jews from his nation in 1290, primarily because of their usury and other abuse of loans at interest, but also because of cases of ritual killing of Christian children by Jews—notably, William of Norwich in 1144 and Hugh of Lincoln in 1255. Jews would not return to England for some 350 years, during which time that nation experienced a true flowering of culture, economy, and political influence around the globe. Meanwhile in Europe, other Jewish expulsions had commenced: France (1306 and 1394), Germany (1348), Hungary (1349), Austria (1421), Lithuania (1445), Provence (1490), Spain (1492), Portugal (1497). But these would only be

---

[20] It is a striking fact that any truly Christian society would prohibit all interest on loans, which would have a vast effect in a modern economy, given that our entire system is predicated on the economic growth brought about by loan-interest. An interest-free economy would be a largely growth-free economy, resulting in stability, sustainability, and fairness.
[21] Hood (1995: 78).

temporary measures, as we know; within two or three centuries the Jews were back, in sufficiently large numbers to cause problems once again.

The first 200 years of the Renaissance saw the peak and then gradual decline of Church authority, and the concurrent rise of local kings, kingdoms, and city-states. The Papal Schism (1378-1417) and charges of internal corruption were early signs of serious problems within the Church. Shortly thereafter, Lorenzo Valla's exposure of the fraudulent 'Donation of Constantine' in 1440 struck another harsh blow at Catholic claims of divine right to governance, which in truth was always at odds with Christian theology.[22] The popes were increasingly seen more as corrupt, power-hungry tyrants than as pious men of God.

Church leaders, then, had to increasingly defend the Faith from critics, including the Jews. In 1458, a preacher in Spain, Alphonso (or Alonso) de Spina (or Espina), said to be a converted Jew, published a defense tract titled *Fortress of Faith*. Part three of that work was titled "Against the Jews," attacking them both on theological grounds and for the growing cases of blood libel that had emerged around Europe, along with a general catalog of Jewish crimes and criminality.[23]

It was in this context that a major thinker and "Christian humanist," Desiderius Erasmus, came to criticize the Jews of Europe. Critical comments began in 1516, at the age of 51, when a letter to a friend remarked that "Judaism [is] the most pernicious plague and bitterest enemy that one can find to the teachings of Christ".[24] He was particularly incensed at ethnic Jews who had nominally converted to Christianity—men like Matthias Adrian and William Pfefferkorn, the latter of which "did more harm to Christendom than the whole cesspool of Jewry." Such men merely "don the mask of a Christian" and use their new-found status to attack prominent Christians, thus effectively benefiting their fellow Jews. Erasmus, in fact, blamed such "converted" Jews, or Conversos, for the growing rift in orthodox Catholicism—a divide that would soon culminate in Martin Luther and the Reformation.

---

[22] The Donation was a document, allegedly written in 315 AD, in which emperor Constantine supposedly handed over the empire to Pope Sylvester I, thus justifying papal rule. In reality it was a forgery composed about the year 750, but which passed as authentic for over eight centuries—until Valla.

[23] For more on de Spina and his work, see Chazan (2016), pp. 190-197.

[24] In Markish (1986), p. 67.

In 1519, Erasmus observed that "there is no people who are farther from God than the Jews".[25] By the 1520s, however, the focus of his critique began to shift from purely theological concerns to more racial or ethnic issues. In 1520, he wrote:

> Certain Jews, half-Jews, and quarter-Jews are getting ever stronger, pushing their way among us, bearing the name of Christian but carrying all Moses in their souls… So they are a particularly dangerous threat to the Christian cause, and profit more from slander than from usury. (p. 77)

Ethnic Jews who pretend they are Christian or (today) White are, thus, more dangerous than ordinary Jewish Jews; the mask or disguise, says Erasmus, heightens and expands their perniciousness. And the danger was certainly growing; in 1526, he expressed the worry that "almost the entire world is seized by Judaism" (p. 83).

Then we find a passage of considerable importance and insight in Erasmus' *Interpretation of Psalm* 85 (1528). There he notes that Jesus, despite condemning the Jews, tolerated them and "summoned them to rebirth" along with the Gentiles. For this reason, Christian people through the ages have also tolerated the Jews, even though they could have, and perhaps should have, done much less:

> The Christian people also tolerate [the Jews], although they revile Christ slanderously and wish ill for all of us, when the Christians could, after all, destroy them without a trace, if they wished. The Jews are insignificantly few in number compared to the Christians; they have no state, no laws, no authority, no ruler, no weapons, no soldiers. They could all be exterminated in a single day, but they are tolerated, in the hope given us by the Apostle Paul, when he wrote to the Romans. The Jews have not stumbled so badly, he says, as to have fallen utterly, and, revealing a mystery, he predicts that when all the pagans enter [the Church], then the

---

[25] Ibid., p. 76.

Jews will change their minds and all Israel will be saved.
(p. 86)

Thus we see that Paul's statement in Romans 11 becomes monumentally important in history; Christians would have long ago done away with the pernicious Jews, were it not for Paul's "mystery": that when all the remaining, pagan Gentiles join the Church, then the Jews will too, and hence "all Israel will be saved."

But all this depends on a benign interpretation of Paul's writing. There is another, less-favorable view, namely, that Paul was a devious liar who, like all other Conversos, only faked his religious beliefs in order to benefit his fellow Jews. And in fact it is there in black and white: Romans 11 opens with Paul asking, "Did God reject his [Jewish] people? By no means!" He then admits his Jewish origins: "I am an Israelite myself, a descendant of Abraham, from the tribe of Benjamin." He then lays out his plan: "I am talking to you Gentiles. Inasmuch as I am the apostle to the Gentiles, I take pride in my ministry in the hope that I may somehow arouse my own people to envy and save some of them." The Jews at that time were brutally oppressed by the Gentile Romans, thus compelling Paul to speak directly to them in order that he might "save" his own people, via a new, Judeo-centric Christian religion. The Jews of Paul's day are currently "hardened" against the Gentiles, but they will soon come around to the Christian strategy: "Israel has experienced a hardening in part until the full number of the Gentiles has come in, and in this way, all Israel will be saved." And that, indeed, was Paul's final aim: to save all Israel, that is, all the Jews; preaching to the Gentiles was always merely a means to that end.

Were it not, then, for a single chapter in one book of the New Testament, we might well not have had any Jews in the world today—and the course of history would have been radically different.

In any event, Erasmus continued to grow more suspicious of Jewish intentions as time went on. In a letter of 1529, when he was 63 years old, he lamented the damage done to a Basel, Switzerland church during one phase of the Reformation:

This is only the beginning. I fear terribly that this [Jewish] pharisaism will be follow by paganism... It seems to me

> that there are many Jews and pagans mixed up in the troubles here, the first of them [the Jews] hating Christ and the others believing in nothing at all. It seems to me that they are dreaming up some sort of new democracy, and the whole business is the work of the sliest possible designs of some people whom no one yet knows precisely. (pp. 87-88)

Again, surreptitious Jews work with others to undermine the Church by bringing about a sort of "democracy" in which they, rather than the religious Gentiles, can exercise power. (One is reminded here of the statement by poet Ezra Pound in the 1930s: "Democracy is currently defined in Europe as a country run by Jews.") Notably, the Jews operate "slyly," such that no one really know who these people are or what exactly they are doing. One gets the distinction impression that little has changed in 400 years.

Finally, in 1536, his last year of life, he issued a full-throated condemnation. Jews are

> envious, stubborn, ungrateful, corrupt, impious, superstitious, arrogant, malicious, suspicious, slanderous, coarse and stupid, savage, rabid, jealous, and of a hopelessly base nature. ... They are despised by all people and [are] pitiful, abject, and sterile.[26]

It is almost as if Erasmus was saving up all his invective for one final thrust at the Jewish enemy of the world.

The Indefatigable Martin Luther

Erasmus was hugely influential throughout Europe of the time, and perhaps his most prominent student was Martin Luther, a man some 20 years his junior. Unlike Erasmus, who never left the Catholic faith, Luther got so disgusted with Church corruption that, in 1517, he posted his famous "95 Theses" which formed the basis for the nascent Protestant movement. By 1520, he could publicly declare the pope to be the Anti-

---

[26] In Falk (1992), p. 53.

christ. He would go on, of course, to found the Lutheran movement as a contrast to the decayed theology of Rome.

Notably, Luther's low opinion of the pope was matched by that of the Jews. In 1541, as he was discoursing on the proper procedure for baptism, he was asked how to baptize a Jew. "If a Jew, not converted at heart, were to ask baptism at my hands, I would take him on to the bridge, tie a stone round his neck, and hurl him into the river; for those wretches are wont to make a jest of our religion".[27] The following year Luther became convinced of the need to write a lengthy critique, for reasons that apparently extended beyond mere religious strife:

> I intend to write against the Jews once again because I hear that some of our lords [nobles] are befriending them. I'll advise them to chase all the Jews out of their land. What reason do they have to slander and insult the dear Virgin Mary as they do? They call her a stinkpot, a hag, a monstrosity. If I were a lord I'd take them by the throat, or they'd have to show cause [why I shouldn't]. They're wretched people. I know of no stronger argument against them than to ask them why they've been in exile so long. (1955: 426)

The result was one of the most notorious religious tracts in history, *On the Jews and Their Lies* (*Von den Jüden und ihren Lügen*). The Jews are an arrogant and obnoxious race, Luther said, whose claim to uniquely divine blessing is as false as it is misguided. As he writes in the Preface, "Those miserable and accursed people" and their "poisonous activities" sought to undermine the Christian faith through their "vile interpretation" of the Bible.[28] Their cause is hopeless; one should not waste time trying to persuade them. In the book, Luther's language is brutal and uncompromising; his frankness and explicitness cannot be overemphasized. The following is a selection of some of his astonishing statements:

---

[27] Luther (1902: 165).
[28] All following quotations and page numbers refer to the recent 2025 edition of *On the Jews and Their Lies* (Clemens & Blair).

- "The sun has never shone on a more bloodthirsty and vengeful people than they are who imagine that they are God's people who have been commissioned and commanded to murder and to slay the Gentiles. In fact, the most important thing that they expect of their Messiah is that he will murder and kill the entire world with their sword." (Part I – p. 22)

- "Therefore, be on your guard against the Jews, knowing that wherever they have their synagogues, nothing is found but a den of devils in which sheer self-glory, conceit, lies, blasphemy, and defaming of God and men are practiced most maliciously and vehemently, just as the devils themselves do." (I – pp. 36-37)

- "They are the circumcised saints who have God's commandments and do not keep them, but are stiff-necked, disobedient, prophet-murderers, arrogant, usurers, and filled with every vice, as the whole of Scripture and their present conduct bear out." (II – p. 72)

- "[B]e on your guard against the Jews, who, as you discover here, are consigned by the wrath of God to the devil, who has not only robbed them of a proper understanding of Scripture, but also of ordinary human reason, shame, and sense, and only works mischief with Holy Scripture through them. Therefore, they cannot be trusted and believed in any other matter either, even though a truthful word may occasionally drop from their lips." (II – pp. 74-75)

- "They alone want to have the Messiah and be masters of the world. The accursed Goyim must be servants, give their desire (that is, their gold and silver) to the Jews, and let themselves be slaughtered like wretched cattle." (II – pp. 76-77)

- "And these dreary dregs, this stinking scum, this dried-up froth, this moldy leaven and boggy morass of Jewry should merit, on the strength of their repentance and righteousness, the empires of the whole world—that is, the Messiah and the fulfillment of the prophecies—though they possess none of the aforementioned items and are nothing but rotten, stinking, rejected dregs of their fathers' lineage!" (II – p. 100)

- "Moreover, they are nothing but thieves and robbers who daily eat no morsel and wear no thread of clothing which they have not stolen and pilfered from us by means of their accursed usury. Thus they live from day to day, together with wife and child, by theft and robbery, as arch-thieves and robbers, in the most impenitent security." (II – pp. 100-101)

- "The Jews have not acquired a perfect mastery of the art of lying; they lie so clumsily and ineptly that anyone who is just a little observant can easily detect it." (II – p. 110)

- "This is to say that he is to kill and exterminate all of us Goyim through their Messiah, so that they can lay their hands on the land, the goods, and the government of the whole world. And now a storm breaks over us with curses, defamation, and derision that cannot be expressed with words. They wish that sword and war, distress and every misfortune may overtake us accursed Goyim." (III – p. 122)

- "No one is holding them here now. The country and the roads are open for them to proceed to their land whenever they wish. If they did so, we would be glad to present gifts to them on the occasion; it would be good riddance. They are a heavy burden, a plague, a pestilence, a sheer misfortune for our country." (III – p. 123)

- "We are at fault in not slaying them." (III – p. 124)

- "Such a desperate, thoroughly evil, poisonous, and devilish lot are these Jews, who for these 1,400 years have been and still are our plague, our pestilence, and our misfortune." (IV – p. 133)

- "That they are venomous, bitter, vindictive, tricky serpents, assassins, and children of the devil, who sting and work harm stealthily wherever they cannot do it openly." (IV – p. 135)

- "Now, let me commend these Jews sincerely to whoever feels the desire to shelter and feed them, to honor them, to be fleeced, robbed, plundered, defamed, vilified, and cursed by them, and to suffer every evil at their hands—these venomous serpents and devil's children, who are the most vehement enemies of Christ our Lord and of us all." (IV – p. 136)

- "They must be driven from our country." (IV – p. 144)

- "If they are caught in the act or charged with something, they are bold enough to deny it impudently, even to the point of death, since they don't regard us worthy of being told the truth. In fact, these holy children of God consider any harm they can wish or inflict on us as a great service to God. Indeed, if they had the power to do to us what we are able to do to them, not one of us would live for an hour." (IV – pp. 144-145)

- "Undoubtedly they do more and viler things than those which we know and discover." (IV – p. 145)

Luther even resurrects, indirectly, the old *foetor Judaicus*: "It serves them right that…they have to look into the devil's black, dark, lying behind, and worship his stench" (III – p. 115). But for a major Christian thinker to say of the Jews, "We are at fault in not slaying them," is so remarkable, so shocking, that one scarcely knows how to respond. It echoes the similar sentiment of Chrysostom, who said the Jews were "fit for slaughter." We can only imagine the depth of feeling that compelled such statements.

On the Jews and Their Lies was written in 1543 when Luther was 60 years old; he would live just three more years. It was one of his last major works, but the views therein were evidently a lifelong conviction. Even some of his earliest writings, such as his lectures on the Psalms dating to 1513 (age 30), include the essence of his later attack. As well his *Lectures on Romans* (1515) reiterates similar concerns. He relented somewhat in a 1523 work, *That Jesus Christ was Born a Jew*, but this seems to have been a minor deviation from his more deeply-held views.

But it is the final quotation (above) that truly strikes a chord in the present day: "undoubtedly they do more and viler things than those which we know and discover." Anyone who follows the news carefully will be astonished at the degree of Jewish malfeasance, how Jews are at the root of so many problems, and that, the more we dig, the more Jewish evil comes to light. However much we know, and however bad we think it is, it is assuredly worse than we think.

CHAPTER 4

BRITISH CRITIQUES,
RENAISSANCE TO 20TH CENTURY

The Jews, the eternal strangers and sojourners...
—P. Johnson (1987: 568)

A Jewish presence existed in England as far back as the time of William the Conqueror, circa 1060. As elsewhere, they quickly established themselves in business, trade, and finance. And as elsewhere, they came into conflict with the local populace for both theological and practical reasons, the latter mostly revolving around usury and tax collection for the royals. On the tax issue, noted British economist William Cunningham (1896: 201) observed that "the Jews served the purpose of a sponge which sucked up the resources of the subjects, and from which their wealth could be easily squeezed into the royal coffers."

Then a more serious incident: In 1255, in the northern English town of Lincoln, a 9-year-old boy named Hugh was found murdered, his body thrown into a well. The body showed signs of ritual murder, and local Jews were charged with the crime. One of them confessed, possibly under torture, that it was Jewish custom to kill a Christian child every year—a variation on the so-called blood libel charge that dates back to Theophrastus' remarks of 310 BC.[1]

The tragedy of "Little St. Hugh" was one in a string of events that led, in 1290, to the expulsion of all Jews from England by Edward I. This was the first such event of the modern era, and foreshadowed those to follow on the Continent over the subsequent two centuries. Unlike the other nations, this one was quite successful; there was almost no Jewish presence in England for more than 350 years.

Hugh's story was also inspiration for Chaucer's "The Prioress's Tale," a chapter in his *Canterbury Tales*, written in the late 1300s. The Prioress recounts the story of an unnamed Christian city in Asia with its

---

[1] See his comments in Chapter One.

own "Jewerye," or Jewish ghetto. The Jews were enclosed there "for foule usure [usury]" and ill-gotten profits. The young son of a local widow takes to singing a Christian hymn as he walks through the town, which offends the Jews. Satan, who "hath in Jues herte [Jew's heart] his wasps nest," incites them to kill the boy:

> Fro thennes forth the Jues han conspired
> This innocent out of this world to chace.
> An homicide therto han they hyred,
> That in an aleye hadde a privee place.

The "cursed Jew" held the boy, "kitte his throte" (slit his throat), and threw him into a pit. Fearing the worst, the distraught widow goes out into the town, and "among the cursed Jues she hym soghte." She finds the body, and the local authorities then sentence the Jews to death. Chaucer concludes the tale with a bleak reminder: "O yonge Hugh of Lyncoln, slayn also / With cursed Jewes, as it is notable."

The Jews had been banished, but English writers were not unfamiliar with the common European attitudes of the time. Shakespeare's *Merchant of Venice*, written about 1598, includes the infamous portrayal of Shylock the Jewish moneylender. Jews were still active in Venice—an eviction order of 1571 was never carried out—but they were publicly stigmatized by distinctive clothing, and were compelled to live in the Jewish ghetto. In the play, Shylock alludes to abuse by Christians: "You call me misbeliever, cut-throat dog, / And spit upon my Jewish gaberdine…" (Act I, sc. III). Launcelot decries his indebtedness, and seeks "to run from this Jew my master"; he adds, "Certainly the Jew is the very devil incarnal" (Act II, sc. II). Later, when the debt is defaulted, Shylock shows no mercy: "Why, this bond is forfeit; / And lawfully by this the Jew may claim / A pound of flesh, to be by him cut off / Nearest the merchant's heart" (Act IV, sc. I). Certainly an unsympathetic portrayal, but likely accurate. Unsurprisingly, Jewish critics continue to condemn the play, even after five centuries. Harold Bloom (1998: 171) declared it "a profoundly anti-Semitic work." More recently, Steve Frank says that it "perpetuates vile stereotypes"; he calls for a 150-year ban on the play, at a minimum.[2] So much for freedom of artistic expression.

By the mid-17th century, Jews were returning to England and lobbying for civil rights. But it wasn't until the notorious "Jew Bill" of 1753 that they were allowed to become naturalized citizens, and full emancipation would not come until the legislative debates of the 1830s and 1840s. Meanwhile, British historians were continually reexamining the Jewish role in history. Already in the 1740s in France, Mirabaud was compiling ancient critiques. In the 1770s, it came to the attention of the influential historian Edward Gibbon, whose monumental work *The History of the Decline and Fall of the Roman Empire* was completed in 1788. In Chapter 15 he undertakes "to inquire by what means the Christian faith obtained so remarkable a victory over the established religions of the earth." He identifies five causes, the first of which was "the zeal of the Jews." Starting from the widespread "religious harmony of the ancient world," Gibbon famously observes that

> a single people refused to join in the common intercourse of mankind. The Jews...emerged from obscurity...and multiplied to a surprising degree... The sullen obstinacy with which they maintained their peculiar rites and unsocial manners seemed to mark them out a distinct species of men, who boldly professed, or who faintly disguised, their implacable hatred to the rest of human-kind. (1788/1974: 3)

Footnotes cite the writings of Tacitus, Diodorus, Dio Cassius, Justin, Juvenal, Cicero, and Philo for justification.[3]

The acquisition of civil rights did not mean the end of anti-Jewish sentiment, even among the more enlightened Brits. William Blake (1757-1827) harbored a kind of "hostility" toward the Jews that found subtle expression in his poems. In *The Marriage of Heaven and Hell*, Blake has a metaphorical discussion with the Jewish prophets Isaiah and Ezekiel, when the latter states that, due to their monotheism, "we [Jews] cursed in

---

[2] *Washington Post*, 28 July 2016.
[3] In fact, their misanthropic characterization of the Jews was much harsher and more widely-acknowledged than Gibbon realized. Recall their remarks in Chapters One and Two.

[God's] name all the deities of surrounding nations" (1982: 39). As a consequence of the Jews' "firm perswasions," "all nations believe the jews code and worship the jews god, and what greater subjection can be?" His *Song of Liberty* recalls an old stereotype, "O Jew, leave counting gold!" (44). And on a number of occasions Blake refers to the "Synagogue of Satan," the standard anti-Jewish epithet of the day. For example, in *Jerusalem* he remarks that man needs a religion, and

> if he has not the Religion of Jesus, he will have the Religion of Satan, & will erect the Synagogue of Satan. ...
> Every Religion that Preaches Vengeance for Sin is the Religion of the Enemy & Avenger...and their God is Satan.[4]

Further such references are found in *The Four Zoas* ("Night the Eighth").

Finally, in his extended commentary on a pro-Christian book, Blake condemns the "Wickedness of the Israelites" for murdering the Canaanites at God's behest. "The Jewish Scriptures...are only an Example of the wickedness & deceit of the Jews" (614). He rails against the "Murderers & Revengers such as the Jews were." In general, "the laws of the Jews were (both ceremonial & real) the basest & most oppressive of human codes" (618). Jesus himself, being divine, could not have been a Jew: "Christ died as an Unbeliever" (614). And indeed, says Blake, he would have no respect at all for him, "if I thought he had been one of those long spindle-nosed rascals".[5]

Blake's contemporary and fellow-poet, Lord Byron, also took a dim view of the Hebrew tribe. In the 100 years since their readmission to England, Jews had become a very prominent minority, rapidly gaining influence in the process. A portion of his political poem, "The Age of Bronze" (1823), was dedicated to this topic:

> How rich is Britain! not indeed in mines,
> Or peace or plenty, corn or oil or wines;

---

[4] (1982: 201). The phrase 'synagogue of Satan' originates in the New Testament, appearing twice in the Book of Revelation (2:9, 3:9). In both instances it is spoken by Jesus himself.

[5] In Shabetai (1995: 139). In fact, Jesus was almost certainly one of those "spindle-nosed rascals."

No land of Canaan, full of milk and honey,
Nor (save in paper shekels) ready money:

But let us not to own the truth refuse,
Was ever Christian land so rich in Jews?

Those parted with their teeth to good King John,
And now, ye kings! they kindly draw your own;

All states, all things, all sovereigns they control,
And waft a loan "from Indus to the pole."

The banker, broker, baron, brethren, speed
To aid these bankrupt tyrants in their need.

Nor these alone; Columbia feels no less
Fresh speculations follow each success;

And philanthropic Israel deigns to drain
Her mild percentage from exhausted Spain.

Not without Abraham's seed can Russia march;
'Tis gold, not steel, that rears the conqueror's arch.

Two Jews, a chosen people, can command
In every realm their scripture-promised land—

Two Jews keep down the Romans, and uphold
The accursed Hun, more brutal than of old;

Two Jews—but not Samaritans—direct
The world, with all the spirit of their sect.

What is the happiness of earth to them?
A congress forms their "New Jerusalem,"

Where baronies and orders both invite—
Oh, holy Abraham! dost thou see the sight?

Thy followers mingling with these royal swine,
Who spit not "on their Jewish gaberdine,"

But honour them as portion of the show—
(Where now, oh Pope! is thy forsaken toe?

Could it not favor Judah with some kicks?
Or has it ceased to "kick against the pricks?")

On Shylock's shore behold them stand afresh,
To cut from nations' hearts their "pound of flesh."

We note that "Columbia" refers to the newly-born American nation; even here, as Sombart wrote, the Jewish financial presence was felt. That the Jews are able to "direct the world" is a reference to the Rothschild banking house, which profited massively from the Napoleonic wars, and by 1815 held decisive control over the financial affairs of both England and France. And of course, the "Jewish gaberdine" and "pound of flesh" come from *Merchant of Venice*.

Mid- to Late-19th Century Views

A notable critique of the mid-century comes, surprisingly, from a Jew himself. Benjamin Disraeli was a prominent British author and politician, eventually rising to become the first Jewish Prime Minister in 1874. Among his more important non-fiction works was the political biography *Lord George Bentinck* (1852), and Chapter 24 attempts to address the reason why the mass of Britons "treat that [Jewish] race as the vilest of generations" (1852/1969: 483). After dismissing the claim that the dispersion of the Jews came as a result of their 'killing Christ,' Disraeli goes on to argue that, in a sense, the Jewish dispersion was well-deserved:

Persecution, in a word, although unjust, may have reduced the modern Jews to a state almost justifying malignant

vengeance. They may have become so odious and so hostile to mankind, as to merit for their present conduct, the
obloquy and ill-treatment of which communities in which
they dwell, and with which they are scarcely permitted to
mingle. (489)

Throughout the great European cities, he adds, Jews "are not the only
people who are usurers, gladiators, and followers of mean and scandalous
occupations…, but considering their general numbers, they contribute perhaps more than their proportion to the aggregate of the vile." Despite
constant persecution, Jews persist. "Obdurate, malignant, odious, and
revolting as the lowest Jew appears to us, he is rarely demoralized." A bit
later he writes of Jewish racial purity, and in fact acknowledges—and
endorses—their self-conception of racial superiority:

[Jews] are a living and the most striking evidence of the
falsity of that pernicious doctrine of modern times, the natural equality of man. … [T]he natural equality of man is
now in vogue, and taking the form of a cosmopolitan fra-
ternity, is a principle which, were it possible to act on it,
would deteriorate the great races and destroy all the genius
of the world. … The native tendency of the Jewish race…is
against the doctrine of the equality of man. (496-497)

Disraeli notes that the Jews "have become remarkable for their accumu-
lated wealth," and he confirms their substantial influence in Europe: "If
the reader throws his eye over the provisional governments of Germany,
and Italy, and even of France, formed at that period, he will recognize
everywhere the Jewish element." The chapter closes by noting that Jesus,
the Jew, has "conquered the Caesars" and "conquered Europe," such that
"the whole of the new world is devoted to the Semitic principle." "Who
can deny," he writes, "that Jesus of Nazareth…is the eternal glory of the
Jewish race?" (507). This, of course, has profound implications; if the
ideology of Jesus, via Paul and the anonymous gospel writers, is the em-
bodiment of the "Semitic principle," and if Christianity is "the eternal
glory of the Jewish race," then today's 2.5 billion Christians are actually

embracing a fundamentally Judaic outlook and morality and are therefore ultimately serving Jewish interests—whether they know it or not.

A few decades later, British writer Laurence Oliphant published a monograph on the need for a Jewish homeland in Palestine: *The Land of Gilead* (1880). Oliphant was no critic of the Jews, and in fact he could be counted as among the earliest so-called Christian Zionists. Thus his reflections on the power of the Jewish community at large are all the more striking. Near the end of his book, he writes,

> And here I would remark that the advantages of an alliance with the Jewish race, to any Power likely to become involved in the impending complications in the East, which may possibly involve a general war, appear to have been altogether overlooked by European statesmen.... The nation that espoused the cause of the Jews and their restoration to Palestine, would be able to rely upon their support in financial operations on the largest scale, upon the powerful influence which they wield in the press of many countries, and on their political cooperation in those countries— which would of necessity tend to paralyze the diplomatic and even hostile action of Powers antagonistic to the one with which they were allied. Owing to the financial, political, and commercial importance to which the Jews have now attained, there is probably no one Power in Europe that would prove so valuable an ally to a nation likely to be engaged in a European war, as this wealthy, powerful, and cosmopolitan race. (1880: 503)

This is a concise description of an integrated and influential world Jewry, one that dominates "the press in many countries" and can thereby mobilize and shape public opinion in a decisive way. On the Continent, this power had already been noted by such figures as Marx, Bauer, Wagner, and Marr, as we will see in the next chapter; but the recognition that it encompassed the Anglo world and beyond was a relatively new development.

The evident power and influence of the Jewish community prompted an impressive 1893 essay by Oxford historian Goldwin Smith, entitled "The Jewish Question." By this time, he had resided in Canada for some

20 years, and with his British connections was well-placed to comment. "Jewish ascendancy," he begins, "form[s] an important feature of the European situation," and is now "beginning to excite attention in America" (1894: 241). He then briefly cites a pro-Jewish article of the previous year in which a British official, Arnold White, describes Jewish influence. A longer excerpt, from the original article, is illuminating:

> Almost without exception, the Press throughout Europe is in Jewish hands, and is largely produced from Jewish brains. International finance is captive to Jewish energy and skill. In England, the fall of the Barings [bank] has left the lonely supremacy of the house of Rothschild, not wholly to its advantage, unchallenged and unassailable. In other walks of life, wherever material comfort and personal safety can be attained by nimble brain, deft finger, or quick imagination, the Jew is found to take the highest place. Medicine, law, surgery, politics, journalism, music and art, are being more and more captained by men of the Jewish race; and it is certain that the process is not on the wane. (White 1892: 696)

Under such circumstance, says Smith, criticism is simply not allowed: "everyone who...fails to show undivided sympathy with the Israelites is set down as a religious persecutor." He proceeds to recount the recent allegations of Russian pogroms, noting the extensive lies and exaggerations reported by western Jews—with claims of financial loss overstated by a factor of 50 or more.

Smith's main argument is that animosity toward Jews stems not from religious differences but from economic and cultural conflicts. "Even in the Middle Ages," he says, "the quarrel was...less religious and more economical or social than is supposed." "In ordinary times the main causes of the hatred of the Jews among the common people appear to have been usury and a social arrogance, which was particularly galling on the part of the alien..." As far back as the late Roman Empire, Jews "were the great slave traders, buying captives from barbarian invaders and probably acting as general brokers of spoils at the same time" (1894: 260). Their wealth grew, and as a result "Judaism is now the great financial power of Europe, that is, it is the greatest power of all." Smith offers some concluding remarks:

> The Jew has thus worn everywhere the unpopular aspect of an intruder, who by his financial skill was absorbing the wealth of the community without adding to it. Not to produce but to make a market of everything has been his general tendency and forte. Among other things he has made a market of war. … He has constantly followed in the wake of armies, making his profit out of the havoc and out of the recklessness of the soldier. … [Judaism has formed] everywhere a nation within the nation, [which] could not possibly fail to lead, as it has led, to mutual hatred and the troubles which ensue. (278, 280)

Regarding a response to this unpleasant situation, Smith unfortunately offers no suggestions.

Into the Twentieth Century: H. G. Wells

British writer H. G. Wells was known for his science fiction, but he wrote in a wide variety of literary genres, and often included insightful social commentary. His novel *Tono-Bungay* (1909) offers this brief observation: "They are a very clever people, the Jews, but not clever enough to suppress their cleverness" (2005: 16). Then came World War I, German defeat, the Treaty of Versailles, and brutal German reparations. Many people—including Henry Ford (see below) and Adolf Hitler—realized that the Jews had a prominent hand in the war, and in the onerous claims on Germany. Such ideas, combined with growing Jewish influence in media and commerce, led Wells and other to continue to speak out.

In a 1919 nonfiction text, *The Outline of History*, Wells examined the origins of Christianity as an outgrowth of Judaism:

> The Jewish idea was and is a curious combination of theological breadth and intense racial patriotism. The Jews looked for a special savior, a Messiah, who was to redeem

mankind by the agreeable process of restoring the fabulous glories of David and Solomon, and bringing the whole world at last under the benevolent but firm Jewish heel. (1971: 585)

In 1933, just as the National Socialists assumed power and began the process of removing Jews from German society, Wells published a realist sci-fi novel, *The Shape of Things to Come*, speculating on future history. Near the end of the work, post-2059 AD, he foresees the following:

There had been a widespread belief in the tenacity and solidarity of Judaism. The Jews had been able to keep themselves a people apart, eating peculiar food and following distinctive religious practices, a nation within the nation, in every state in the world. They had been a perpetual irritant to statesmen, a breach in the collective solidarity everywhere. They had played a peculiar in-and-out game of social relationship. One could never tell whether a Jew was being a citizen or whether he was being just a Jew. They married, they traded preferentially. They had their own standards of behaviour. Wherever they abounded, their peculiarities aroused bitter resentment.

It might have been supposed that a people so widely dispersed would have developed a cosmopolitan mentality and formed a convenient linking organization for many world purposes, but their special culture of isolation was so intense that this they neither did nor seemed anxious to attempt. After the World War [One], the orthodox Jews played but a poor part in the early attempts to formulate the Modern State, being far more preoccupied with a dream called Zionism, the dream of a fantastic independent state all of their own in Palestine, which according to their Babylonian legend was the original home of all this synthesis of Semitic-speaking peoples. Only a psycho-analyst could begin to tell for what they wanted this Zionist state. It emphasized their traditional willful separation from the main body of mankind. It irritated the world against them, subtly and incurably. (1933/1945: 383)

Three years later Wells penned a sprawling and pessimistic commentary on modern life, in the face of a looming militarism in Europe—*Anatomy of Frustration*. Here he explicitly remarks on the German program for dealing with the Jewish Question, beginning with the usual charges against the Jews:

[The Jews] are brighter and cleverer with money. They get, they permeate, they control. The non-Jewish populations amidst which they live do not admit any inferiority to them; they feel that this successful Jewish concentration is made at the expense of broader and finer interests, of leisure, brooding contemplation and experiment. But if they are to hold their own against the biological pressure of the Jew they must drop these alleged broader and finer interests, whatever they are, and concentrate on the struggle for possession. The Jew makes the biological pace for them at a lower level, unless they impose a handicap on him or resort periodically to some form of pogrom. ...

[This indictment] is the very core of the Jewish trouble. Are the Jews more pushful than non-Jews? Does their energy in the attainment of opportunity block the way to slower but sounder and deeper accomplishment? ... [W]e are dealing here with a *distinctive tradition of behavior* that taints, hampers, and frustrates much human effort. The Jew is not a good citizen in this sense, that he does not give a whole-hearted allegiance to the institutions, conventions and collective interests and movements of the community in which he finds himself. Neither is he creative in the common interest. He is an alien with an alien mentality, and the achievement of "spoiling the Egyptians" lurks at the fountain-head of his ideology. His acquisitive keenness, his concentration upon attainment, his disregard of sentimental and ultimate standards, is in a large part due to the way in which his alien tradition releases him from "playing the game" of the community life simply and completely.

You may repudiate and fight against the clumsy re-vengefulness, the plunderings, outrages and fantastic intim-idations of the Nazi method, but that does not close the Jewish problem for you. It merely brings you back to the fundamental age-long problem of this nation among the na-tions, this in-and-out mentality, the essential parasitism of the Jewish mycelium upon the social and cultural organ-isms in which it lives. (1936: 137-138)

Wells then adds, pointedly, "This is a problem for Jews to consider and solve for themselves."

Another reference came two years later, in a short essay of late 1938. Titled "The Future of the Jews," Wells begins the piece with a wry observation on Jewish self-centeredness:

I met a Jewish friend of mind the other day and he asked me, "What is going to happen to the Jews?" I told him I had ra-ther he had asked me a different question, "What is going to happen to mankind?" "But *my* people—" he began. "That," said I, "is exactly what is the matter with them".[6]

He then recalls the circumstances of World War I. It was supposed to be "a War to End War," from which would arise a lasting era of world peace:

But throughout those tragic and almost fruitless four years of war, [Israel] Zangwill and the Jewish spokesmen were most elaborately and energetically demonstrating that they cared not a rap for the troubles and dangers of English, French, Germans, Russians, Americans or of any other people but their own.[7]

---

[6] Reprinted in Wells (1939: 53). Original appeared in *Sunday Chronicle*, De-cember 1938.
[7] Zangwill was a noted British-Jewish writer and political activist.

A following passage is as relevant today as it was in 1938: "there is a growing irritation at the killing and wounding of British soldiers and Arabs in pitched battles fought because of the Zionist ideal." The "national egotism" of the Jews arises "because they are haunted by a persuasion that they are a chosen people with distinctive privileges over their Gentile fellow-creatures." This Jewish "irrational nationalism" has led to grave injustice: "they have treated the inhabitants of Palestine practically as non-existent people, and yet these same Arabs are a people more purely Semitic than themselves" (1939b: 59). The Jews, says Wells, are not exceptional; they are not pure, not "chosen." The solution to the Jewish problem is a radical "emancipation"—of truth. And the burden for this lies on their shoulders:

> There are thousands of Jewish writers, professors, philosophers, journalists…who might contribute enormously more than they do now to the release and enlightenment of mankind—if only they would forget they are Jews and remember that they are men. (62)

These ideas are reiterated in one of Wells' later nonfiction works, the 1939 book *The Fate of Homo Sapiens* (an edited and sanitized version was published in the USA as *The Fate of Man*). As a sociological study of the future, this book envisions the nature of coming civilization and the various factors influencing or hindering it. Chapter 12 is of particular interest: "The Jewish Influence." Here, Wells elaborates on various negative Jewish qualities, things he believes are impediments to world peace.

The chief problem, says Wells, is the Jewish doctrine of chosenness ("the Lord your God has chosen you to be a people for his own possession, out of all the peoples that are on the face of the Earth"; Deut 7:6). The Jews, of course, wrote that for themselves, and thus it is an entirely self-serving statement—a kind of pathological megalomania. It is this doctrine that "constitutes the Jewish problem." "The whole [Jewish] question turns upon the Chosen People idea," which effectively constitutes "a conspiracy against the rest of the world." Of course: if Jews are "chosen" then everyone else, of necessity, is "unchosen," and thus second- or third-rate, at best. Indeed, the indictment against the Jewish community is that their religion of a Chosen People takes this universal human vice, justifies it, and stimulates it to the form of a persistent organized attitude of self-exclusion from the common fellowship of the world.

This, repeats Wells, is the root of the problem and in itself explains the historical resistance against Jews: "Gentile intolerance is a response to the cult of the Chosen People." The problem, therefore, lies in the Jewish self-chosen mindset, not their Gentile persecutors.

Especially problematic is the Zionist movement. But for a people with a "Chosen" mindset, says Wells, such a project was doomed to failure from the start: "to plant themselves massively in any particular area was to invite a wholesale disaster." And indeed, from 1948 onward, it has certainly been one continuous disaster in the Middle East; one need only witness the ongoing genocidal actions in Gaza to see the concrete manifestation of the doctrine of chosenness.[8]

Wells' British contemporary, George Bernard Shaw, has acquired, in recent years, a reputation as an anti-Semite, but, absurdly, this is based largely on just one or two passing comments. In 1932 Shaw was cornered by a Jewish writer for *The American Hebrew*, looking for sympathetic praise for his beleaguered people. Shaw's reply closely mirrors Wells'—though predating it by six years:

> This craving for bouquets by Jews is a symptom of racial degeneration. The Jews are worse than my own people, the Irish, at it. Those Jews who still want to be the chosen race—chosen by the late Lord Balfour—can go to Palestine and stew in their own juice. The rest had better stop being Jews and start being human beings.[9]

The continuation of the statement, always omitted from popular sources, shows the broader context: "The day of races and nations is over. The

---

[8] The full chapter by Wells is reproduced in Dalton, ed. (2025).
[9] Shaw (1932: 20). The magazine issue is dated 22 October, but popular sources consistently misdate the publication as 12 October.

future belongs to the citizens of the world who know they are no better than other people."

Churchill Speaks his Mind

Consider, now, Winston Churchill. On 8 February 1920, while serving as Secretary of State for War, Churchill published a notorious article, "Zionism versus Bolshevism." After noting that both "the Christ and the Antichrist" seem destined to arise from the Jews, he contrasts the "honorable and useful" Jews in Russia to "the schemes of the International Jews".[10] Churchill continues:

> The adherents of this sinister confederacy are mostly men reared up among the unhappy populations of countries where Jews are persecuted on account of their race. ... This movement among the Jews is not new. From the days of Spartacus-Weishaupt to those of Karl Marx, and down to Trotsky (Russia), Bela Kun (Hungary), Rosa Luxembourg (Germany), and Emma Goldman (United States), this world-wide conspiracy for the overthrow of civilization and for the reconstitution of society on the basis of arrested development, of envious malevolence, and impossible equality, has been steadily growing. It played, as a modern writer, Mrs. Webster, has so ably shown, a definitely recognizable part in the tragedy of the French Revolution.[11] It has been the mainspring of every subversive movement during the 19th century; and now at last this band of extraordinary personalities from the underworld of the great cities of Europe and America have gripped the Russian people by the hair of their heads and have become practically the undisputed masters of that enormous empire.
>
> There is no need to exaggerate the part played in the creation of Bolshevism and the actual bringing about of the Russian Revolution by these international and for the most

---

[10] In Brenner (2002: 25). Also reproduced in full in Dalton, ed. (2025).
[11] Nesta Webster was a British writer and historian. Her books include *The French Revolution* (1919) and *The Cause of World Unrest* (1920).

part atheistical Jews. It is certainly a very great one; it probably outweighs all others. With the notable exception of Lenin, the majority of the leading figures are Jews.[12]

Moreover, the principal inspiration and driving power comes from the Jewish leaders. Thus Tchitcherin, a pure Russian, is eclipsed by his nominal subordinate Litvinoff, and the influence of Russians like Bukharin or Lunacharski cannot be compared with the power of Trotsky, or of Zinovieff, the Dictator of the Red Citadel (Petrograd), or of Krassin or Radek—all Jews. In the Soviet institutions the predominance of Jews is even more astonishing. And the prominent, if not indeed the principal, part in the system of terrorism applied by the Extraordinary Commissions for Combating Counter-Revolution has been taken by Jews, and in some notable cases by Jewesses.

The same evil prominence was obtained by Jews in the brief period of terror during which Bela Kun ruled in Hungary. The same phenomenon has been presented in Germany (especially in Bavaria), so far as this madness has been allowed to prey upon the temporary prostration of the German people. Although in all these countries there are many non-Jews every whit as bad as the worst of the Jewish revolutionaries, the part played by the latter in proportion to their numbers in the population is astonishing.

Thus the Jews are the agitators and subversives, the revolutionaries—the "ferment of decomposition," as Mommsen put it.[13] Evidently this was a prominent view in the aftermath of WWI: the "international Jew" was indeed seen as a threat to civilized government.

Even as he accepted help from his Jewish friends and allies, Churchill evidently harbored concerns about them—right up to the eve of WW2. In a recently-discovered 1937 essay, "How the Jews can Combat Persecution," he argues that Jews are, in part, to blame for their own predicament. "It would be easy," he said, "to ascribe it [anti-Semitism] to

---

[12] Lenin was in fact one-quarter Jewish; see Martin Gilbert (*Churchill and the Jews*, 2007, p. 37).
[13] See Chapter 6.

the wickedness of the persecutors, but that does not fit all the facts. ... These facts...should be pondered especially by the Jews themselves. For it may be that, unwittingly, they are inviting persecution—that they have been partly responsible for the antagonism from which they suffer." He continues:

> The central fact which dominates the relations of Jew and non-Jew is that the Jew is 'different.' He looks different. He thinks differently. He has a different tradition and background. He refuses to be absorbed. In every country, the Jews form a distinct and separate community—a little state within the state.
>
> The Jew in England is a representative of his race. Every Jewish money lender recalls Shylock and the idea of the Jews as usurers. And you cannot reasonably expect a struggling clerk or shopkeeper, paying 40 or 50 percent interest on borrowed money to a 'Hebrew bloodsucker,' to reflect that, throughout long centuries, almost every other way of life was closed to Jewish people...[14]

To date only a few portions of the whole piece have been released to the public; evidently the remainder is a bit too much for people to swallow.

---

[14] Quotations taken from various news reports, e.g. *The Telegraph* (UK), dated 11 Mar 2007.

CHAPTER 5

MODERN 'ANTI-SEMITISM' IN FRANCE AND GERMANY

Having now covered British criticisms from the modern era up through the early 20th century, we may now review what may loosely be called 'modern anti-Semitism' in the Continent, specifically in France and Germany. Of particular note is that, as this was the era of the Enlightenment and of a new humanism, the critiques shift markedly from a religious to a secular perspective. This shift is central to present-day attitudes and conflicts, most of which are non-religious in character, and thus it is of prime importance to the contemporary world.

Following their expulsion in the 14th century, Jews began returning to France in the early 1600s, primarily to Alsace and Lorraine. They quickly took up dominant positions in commerce and finance, such that by the early 1700s, notable French intellectuals were beginning to express concern. Among the earliest was the political philosopher Charles-Louis Montesquieu, whose *Lettres persanes* (1721) offered passing commentary. Jewish communities around the world were very much alike, he said; "Know that wherever there is money there are Jews".[1] Repeating an ancient charge, Montesquieu added that, of the supposedly learned rabbis, there was "[not] one among them of even a minor order of genius."

Writing in the 1740s, Jean-Baptiste de Mirabaud composed his *Opinions des anciens sur les Juifs* (Ancient Opinions on the Jews). Employing, for the first time in the modern era, passages such as those examined earlier, Mirabaud argued that ancient scholars developed a well-justified animus towards Jewry:

> You will therefore see from this that, a long time before they had brought down upon themselves this curse, which is now regarded as the cause of their wretchedness, [the Jews] were generally hated and generally despised in every

---

[1] In Hertzberg (1968: 275).

country which knew them: after which you will agree that
there is no mention of them in the old books except in connection with this contempt, and in relation to the general
aversion felt for them…

Not only did all the nations despise the Jews; they even
hated them and believed that they were as justified in hating as
in despising them. They were hated because they were known
to hate other men; they were despised because they were
seen observing customs which were thought ridiculous.[2]

Eighteenth century writer and philosopher Denis Diderot had similar thoughts. The Jews were taught by the Talmud, he said, "to steal the
goods of Christians, to regard them as savage beasts, to push them in a
precipice…to kill them with impunity and to utter every morning the
most horrible imprecations against them".[3] The mutual animosity re-
quired that they be held apart from the public at large—"This people
should be kept separate from others," he wrote in 1763.[4] Five years later,
in his *La Moisade*, Diderot attacked both the Old Testament and present-
day Jews who sustained that mythology: "And you, angry and brutish
people, vile and vulgar men, slaves worthy of the yoke which you
bear…go, take back your books and remove yourselves from me".[5] In
his famous *Encyclopédie*, in an article on Judaism, he added that, among
the Jews,

[one does not find] any rightness of thought, any exactness
in reasoning or precision of style, in a word, any of that
which ought to characterize a healthy philosophy. One
finds among them, on the contrary, only a confused mé-
lange of the principles of reason and revelation, a preten-
tious and often impenetrable obscurity, principles that lead
to fanaticism, blind respect for the authority of the rabbis

---

[2] In Poliakov (1965: 119).
[3] In Barzilay (1956: 254). For an excellent analysis of the Talmud and its
related document, the Shulchan Aruch, see E. Bischoff, *The Book of the
Shulchan Aruch* (2023).
[4] In Hertzberg (1968: 312).
[5] In Hertzberg (1968: 282).

and for antiquity, in a word, all the faults that mark an ignorant and superstitious people.[6]

Jean-Jacques Rousseau was also appalled by the crude partisan theology of the Old Testament. Speaking to the ancient Jews, he said, "[You]
paint us a God, angry, jealous, vengeful, partial, hating men, a God of
war and battles... Your God is not ours. He who begins by selecting a
chosen people, and proscribing the rest of mankind, is not our common
father..." (1769).[7] Such men were "the vilest of peoples"; one is aghast
at "the baseness of this people, incapable of any virtue," a race that constituted "the vilest people perhaps who existed then." Later, in a piece of
backhanded praise for Moses, Rousseau wrote that the Jews were originally "a swarm of wretched fugitives, without arts, without weapons,
without talents, without virtues, without courage..." To maintain their
identity, Moses gave the Hebrew tribe "customs and practices which are
incompatible with those of other nations...to render it always a foreigner
amongst other men." To this day, the Jewish race displays a dogged persistence and adherence to its law, such that it "will last as long as the world,
despite the hatred and persecution of the rest of the human race" (1772).[8]
    Working about the same time as Rousseau, Baron d'Holbach—a ma-
jor figure among Enlightenment thinkers—unleashed a blistering attack on
the Jews. In his *Ecce Homo* of 1770 he made the following observations:

> [When] we cast our eyes over the history of the Jews...we
> are forced to acknowledge, that this people were at all
> times the blindest, the stupidest, the most credulous, the
> most superstitious, and the most puerile that ever appeared
> on the Earth. ... [By Mosaic Law,] the people of God were
> kept in a profound ignorance; in an abject superstition; in
> an unsocial and savage aversion for the rest of mankind; in
> an inveterate hatred of other forms of worship... [T]he
> Jewish people distinguished themselves only by massacres,
> unjust wars, cruelties, usurpations, and infamies...[9]

---

[6] In Hertzberg (1968: 311-312).
[7] In Poliakov (1965: 102).
[8] In Poliakov (1965: 103).
[9] (1770/1813: 23-26).

The Jews, "the most unfortunate people that ever existed...lived continually in the midst of calamities, and were, more than all other nations, the sport of frightful revolutions." The theme continues two years later in *Good Sense* (1772: 147): "Shall we find in Jehovah a model for our conduct? This is a truly savage god, made for a stupid, cruel, and immoral people; he is always furious, breathes nothing but vengeance, commands carnage, theft, and unsociability." And in his *Superstition in All Ages* d'Holbach writes that "Moses was but an Egyptian schismatic" who was little more than a leader of outlaws. "If we consult Tacitus and many other celebrated historians, in regard to Moses and his nation, we shall see that they are considered as a horde of thieves and bandits" (1771/1920: 291). D'Holbach accepts the story of the Jews' human sacrifices, and remarks that, according to prophecy, they should be "the most victorious of all the people of earth." But this was not reality: "And even now the remainder of this unfortunate nation is looked upon as the vilest and most contemptible of all the earth, having no country, no dominion, no superiority".[10]

Monsieur Voltaire Speaks

But the preeminent French critic was surely Voltaire. Throughout his long career, he castigated the Jews at every opportunity, employing all the charges of his fellow countrymen, and more. As early as 1722 he wrote of "the facility which the Jews have for being admitted and expelled everywhere" (Letter to Dubois).[11] They have no loyalty but to themselves, and to riches: "a Jew belongs to no land other than the one where he makes money; can he not just as easily betray the king for the emperor as the emperor for the king?" But this was a mere prelude.

Voltaire's famous *Philosophical Dictionary* first appeared in 1745, containing several entries on Jews, Judaism, and Judeo-Christianity. Some passages from the entry 'Jews' give the flavor of the piece:

> It is certain that the Jewish nation is the most singular that
> the world has ever seen, and...in a political view, the most
> contemptible of all... [T]he Hebrews have ever been vagrants,

---

[10] (1771/1920: 320, 322).
[11] In Hertzberg (1968: 135).

or robbers, or slave, or seditious. They are still vagabonds upon the earth, and abhorred by men, yet affirming that heaven and earth and all mankind were created for them alone. … You ask, what was the philosophy of the Hebrews? The answer will be a very short one—they had none. Their legislator [Moses] himself does not anywhere speak expressly of the immortality of the soul, nor of the rewards of another life. …

It is commonly said that the abhorrence in which the Jews held other nations proceeded from their horror of idolatry; but it is much more likely that the manner in which they, at the first, exterminated some of the tribes of Canaan, and the hatred which the neighboring nations conceived for them, were the cause of this invincible aversion. As they knew no nations but their neighbors, they thought that in abhorring them they detested the whole earth, and thus accustomed themselves to be the enemies of all men. … [The ancient Jews'] stay in Babylon and Alexandria…formed the people to no art, save that of usury.

The entry comes to a striking conclusion:

In short, we find in them only an ignorant and barbarous people, who have long united the most sordid avarice with the most detestable superstition and the most invincible hatred for every people by whom they are tolerated and enriched. Still, we ought not to burn them.[12]

Later writings continued in the same vein. His 1756 *Essai sur les moeurs* (Essay on Morals) addressed the reason for the near-universal dislike of the Jews: "It is the inevitable result of their laws; they either had to conquer everybody or be hated by the whole human race"[13] —though one wonders if this is truly an either/or proposition. Voltaire continues:

---

[12] In Levy (1991: 39-41).
[13] In Hertzberg (1968: 302).

The Jewish nation dares to display an irreconcilable hatred against all nations, and revolts against all masters; always superstitious, always greedy for the good of others, always barbarous—cringing in misfortune, and insolent in prosperity.[14]

And the fundamental reason? "Money was the object of their conduct at all times."

A 1761 essay attacks the ancient Hebrews and their sorry state of social and intellectual development, and makes a sarcastic allusion to the old idea of a diseased people: "It was only in the matter of lice that they were outdone; for that reason it has accurately been said that the Jews know more than any other people about this profession".[15] Of the Old Testament, it "prophesied on a hundred occasions that they would be the masters of the world: however, they never possessed more than a tiny corner of the Earth for a few years; today they haven't even one village of their own."

Stinging comments continued to flow from him over the years:

- "The Jews have never invented anything" (1767). Indeed, they are "plagiarists in everything."

- "You [Jews] are calculating animals, try to be thinking animals" (1770).

- "[You] seem to be to be the maddest of the lot. ... You have surpassed all nations in impertinent fables, in bad conduct, and in barbarism. You deserve to be punished, for this is your destiny" (1772).

- "[T]hese circumcised Jews [are] the greatest scoundrels who have ever sullied the face of the globe" (1773).

---

[14] In Chamberlain (1899/1968: 347).
[15] In Katz (1980: 42).

- And in the final year of his life: "If we must talk of Jewry, we must state that they were a wretched Arabic tribe without art or science, hidden in a small, hilly, and ignorant land..." (1776).[16]

But it was one particular warning by Voltaire that weighs heavily upon us today. In 1771 he wrote:

> [The Jews] are, all of them, born with raging fanaticism in their hearts, just as the Bretons and Germans are born with blond hair. I would not be in the least bit surprised if these people would not someday become deadly to the human race.[17]

Looking back over the past 200 years, and seeing the prominent Jewish hand in slavery, war, genocide, oppression, governmental corruption, rampant capitalism, cultural degradation, financial fraud, environmental destruction...and consider the price humanity has paid for these things, and the price we have yet to pay—*deadly to the human race*. Who shall dispute him?

Finally, we cannot leave the French without hearing from Napoleon. A pragmatic leader, Napoleon sought to resolve the Jewish problem by fully integrating them into Christian society—in effect, making them disappear as a people. This, he thought, would mitigate the damage that had been historically caused by the 'accursed race':

> I do not intend to rescue that race, which seem to have been the only one excluded from redemption, from the curse with which it is smitten, but I would like to put it in a position where it is unable to propagate the evil...[18]

Then in a Council Meeting of 30 April 1806, he was even blunter:

---

[16] In Chamberlain (1899: 347), Poliakov (1965: 89, 89), Hertzberg (1968: 301, 284-285, 304), respectively.

[17] In Hertzberg (1968: 300).

[18] In Poliakov (1965: 226).

The French government cannot watch with indifference as a [Jewish] nation vilified, degraded, and capable of every baseness, monopolizes the two beautiful administrative departments of ancient Alsace; the Jews must be considered as a nation and not as a [religious] sect. It is a nation within the nation. I would like to remove from them, at least for a certain time, the right to take mortgages, for it is too humiliating for the French nation to find itself at the mercy of this vilest nation. Entire villages have been expropriated by the Jews; they have replaced feudalism; they are veritable flocks of crows. ...

It would be dangerous to let the keys of France—Strasbourg and Alsace—fall into the hands of a population of spies who are not attached to the country. In the past, Jews could not even stay overnight in Strasbourg. It will perhaps be appropriate to decree today that there must not be more than 50,000 Jews in the upper and lower Rhine; more than this number and they would spread at will into the rest of France.[19]

And then again in the same forum, one month later:

From the time of Moses, the Jewish nation has been constituted in a usurious and oppressive way. It is not the same with the Christians; usurers are the exception among them and have a bad reputation. ...

I state again that people do not complain of the Protestants or the Catholics in the same way that they do of the Jews. It seems that the evil committed by the Jews comes not from individuals but from the constitution of these people themselves; they are caterpillars, locusts that ravage France.[20]

---

[19] Cited by P. de Lagarde in *Jews and Indo-Germanics* (1887); reproduced in Dalton, ed. (2025), p. 98.
[20] Ibid., p. 99.

Lastly, a familiar critique, offered in an 1808 letter to his brother Jerome:

> I have undertaken to reform the Jews, but I have not en-
> deavored to draw more of them into my realm. Far from
> that, I have avoided doing anything which could show any
> esteem for the most despicable of mankind. (Bonaparte
> 1898: 71)

German Critics: Kant to Schopenhauer

As we saw, the German tradition of Jewish criticism began with Martin Luther in the 16th century, but then took a back seat to the French for more than two centuries. It reemerged in the late 1700s with two of the greatest names in German philosophy, Kant and Hegel. Kant's anti-Jewish stance seems to have surfaced late in life, well after he composed his three famous philosophical Critiques. A small booklet of 1793, *Religion within the Limits of Reason Alone*, laid out an influential history and philosophy of religion. Of the Jewish religion, Kant wrote, "Judaism is really not a religion at all but merely a union of a number of people who…formed themselves into a commonwealth under purely political laws" (1960: 116). This is so because the laws of Moses aim not at God or the fate of the soul, but rather "are directed to absolutely nothing but outer [i.e. physical] observance." Religion is nonexistent if it "involves no belief in a future life," and therefore "Judaism, which, when taken in its purity is seen to lack this belief, is not a religious faith at all." As orig-inally constituted, Judaism is found to

> exclude from its communion the entire human race, on the
> ground that it was a special people chosen by God for Him-
> self—[an exclusiveness] which showed enmity toward all
> other peoples and which, therefore, evoked the enmity of
> all. (ibid.: 117)

A passing comment of interest occurred a year later, in a letter to K. Reinhold of 28 March 1794. Kant explains his reticence at critiquing and judging the philosophical views of others, in this case those of the Jewish thinker Salomon Maimon. He himself is uncomfortable doing so, but

"Jews always like to do that sort of thing, to gain an air of importance for themselves at someone else's expense" (1967: 212).

One of Kant's last major works was the book *Streit der Fakultäten* (Conflict of the Faculties), of 1798. Amidst a general sociological analysis of religion, he remarks that the Jewish prophets constructed an untenable 'state' that would inevitably fail:

> As national leaders they had loaded their constitution with so much ecclesiastical freight, and civil freight tied to it, that their state became utterly unfit to subsist of itself, and especially unfit to subsist together with neighboring nations. (1979: 143)

—an observation that bodes ill for the present state of Israel. The best solution, he thought, was for Judaism to die a quiet death and to adopt the moral teachings of Christianity. Kant's choice of words here is striking, and unintentionally prescient: "the euthanasia of Judaism" (*Die Euthanasie des Judenthums*). As he says, "The euthanasia of Judaism is pure moral religion, freed from all the ancient statutory teachings…" (ibid.: 95).

A smaller work of the same year, *Anthropology*, includes a lengthy footnote on the "Palestinians" (i.e. Jews from Palestine). Early in the book, Kant (1978: 33) criticizes any system of "commandments involving activity which accomplishes nothing, like those upon which Judaism is built." This eventually leads to a discussion of the ethics of deception, and further observations on the Hebrew tribe. The footnote itself is scathing, and brutally on the mark:

> The Palestinians [Jews], living among us, or at least the greatest number of them, have, through their usurious spirit since their exile, received the not-unfounded reputation of deceivers. It seems strange to think of a nation of deceivers; but it is just as strange to think of a nation made up of nothing but merchants, which are united for the most part by an old superstition that is recognized by the government under which they live. They do not seek any civil honor, but rather wish to compensate their loss by profitably outwitting the very people among whom they find protection, and

even to make profit from their own kind. It cannot be otherwise with a whole nation of merchants, who are nonproductive members of society (for example, the Jews in Poland).

Their condition, sanctioned by ancient precepts and recognized even by us, cannot be altered by us without serious consequences, even though they have made the saying "buyer beware" the supreme principle of morality in their dealings with us. ...

[T]hese merchants, after the destruction of their city [Jerusalem], were able to migrate gradually into far-distant lands (in Europe) taking language and religion with them, maintaining their connection with each other, and finding security in whatever countries they went to because of their profitable bargaining. Therefore, we may suppose that their dispersion throughout the world, with their unity in religion and language, must not be attributed to a *curse* that had been inflicted upon this people. On the contrary, the dispersion must be considered as a *blessing* [to them], especially since the wealth of the Jews, if we think of them as individuals, apparently exceeds per capita that of any other nation at the present time. (1978: 101-102)

Note: This was not personal animus, but *considered philosophical opinion*. The Jews, a "nation of merchants and deceivers," out to scam the very people who gave them refuge, resulting in massive accumulation of wealth... Little has changed in 200 years.

In his public lectures at Königsberg University, Kant was more informal but no less pointed. A little-known compilation of several of these talks, published as *Lectures on Ethics*, includes four relevant comments. Speaking on the lack of moral courage involved with lying, Kant said, "Every coward is a liar; Jews, for example, not only in business, but also in common life. It is hardest of all to judge Jews; they are cowards" (1997: 27). Elaborating on the virtues of religious diversity, he observed that, for most religions this would promote social goodwill and tolerance. However: "To be sure, were the principles, if pursued, to be averse to the state, as with the Jews, for example, who are permitted by the Talmud to practice deceit, then the natural feeling rectifies this false article of religion"

(34). Later Kant examined the merits and demerits of in-group favoritism, and especially how this can easily lead to lack of general good will:

> *Esprit de corps* [of one's own social or ethnic group] leads the disposition away from objective moral principles [of goodwill toward all]. [N]or can it ever be otherwise among the Jews that all estimation for other men, who are not Jews, is totally lost, and goodwill is reduced merely to love of their own tribe, under which they are wont to cherish one another according to the *principia* adopted, and receive the more credit, the more the agent approaches to a maximum of expediency, deals falsely, is lucky in turning a profit, or possesses cleverness, cunning, and craft. (406)

Finally, Kant reaffirms the age-old problem of monotheism: "The Jews …despised the maxims of all other religions, since it was they who were uniquely in the possession of a deity, who alone could rank as God, and for whose sake they believed themselves obligated to hate all other deities" (442).

Hegel's critique, by comparison, was rather milder but just as insightful. The bulk of his comments are found in a 1796 composition "The Spirit of Christianity and its Fate." The opening section, titled "The Spirit of Judaism," opens with the notion that Abraham, as "the true progenitor of the Jews," changed history by "regulating the entire fate of his prosperity" (1975: 182). Central to the Jewish worldview was the idea that "the human race had in her…the most destructive, invincible, irresistible hostility; in her fury she spared nothing; she…poured savage devastation over everything." The world was a hostile place, and "nature had to be mastered." The picture is bleak:

> [Abraham] was a stranger on earth, a stranger to the soil and to men alike. Among men he always was and remained a foreigner… The whole world Abraham regarded as simply his opposite; if he did not take it to be a nullity, he looked on it as sustained by the God who was alien to it. … [A]nd since [God's] divinity was rooted in his contempt for the whole world, he remained [God's] only favorite. (186-188)

This produced a people with a grudge against the world, a race that held a malicious, stealthy contempt for other nations. Their enemies "are conquered by an invisible attack," unseen, subterranean. Indeed, "the only act Moses reserved for the Israelites was…to borrow with deceit and repay confidence with theft" (190).

This leads, Hegel said, to a brutish way of life: "Where there is universal enmity, there is nothing left save physical dependence, an animal existence which can be assured only at the expense of all other existence, and which the Jews took as their domain." Judaism was defined by its enemy status; the Jews *needed* enemies to survive as a people. Thus, "the subsequent circumstances of the Jewish people, up to the mean, abject, wretched circumstances in which they still are today, have all of them been simply consequences and elaborations of their original fate" (199). The "soul of the Jewish nationality" is equated with the *"odium generis humani"* (hatred of mankind)—recalling that famous phrase of Tacitus. The section closes with this reflection:

> The great tragedy of the Jewish people…can arouse neither terror nor pity…; it can arouse horror alone. The fate of the Jewish people is the fate of Macbeth who stepped out of nature itself, clung to alien Beings, and so in their service had to trample and slay everything holy in human nature… (204-205)

A cruel fate for the Jews, and for all who are drawn into their circle.

Around the same time, near the turn of the 19th century, other German philosophers were compelled by social conditions to comment. Johann Fichte was concerned primarily about the political ramifications of a growing Jewish subculture within German society. His first major book, *Contributions to the Correction of the Public's Judgment concerning the French Revolution* (1793), addressed the pressing "Jewish Question" of the day: whether or not the Jews should have full civil rights and legal equality. It was an urgent matter. They had just won emancipation in France in 1791, the first country to do so. The number of German Jews was growing, and their inbred culture was on the verge of becoming a "state within a state"—and not only in Germany:

Throughout almost all the countries of Europe there is spreading a mighty hostile state that is at perpetual war with all other states, and in many of them imposes fearful burdens on the citizens: it is the Jews. I do not think, as I hope to show subsequently, that this state is fearful—not because it forms a separate and solidly united state but because this state is founded on the hatred of the whole human race... In a state where the absolute monarch cannot take from me my paternal hut and where I can defend my rights against the all-powerful minister, the first Jew who likes can plunder me with impunity. This you see and cannot deny, and you utter sugary words of tolerance and of the rights of man and civil rights, all the time wounding in us the *primary* rights of man. ...

Do you not remember the state within the State? Does the thought not occur to you that if you give to the Jews, who are citizens of a state more solid and more powerful than any of yours, civil rights in your states, they will utterly crush the remainder of your citizens?[21]

The only answer for Fichte was expulsion, or 'ex-termination': literally, the casting out of a people beyond the borders. "To protect ourselves against them I see no other way than to conquer for them their promised land and see them all there".[22] His plea went unanswered. The Prussian Jews received their emancipation in 1812; those in Württemberg in 1826; and all remaining German Jews were fully integrated upon German unification in 1870. Fichte's fellow citizens would live to regret this development.

Another influential figure, Johann Herder, published his *Reflections on the Philosophy of the History of Mankind* in 1791. This important and widely-read work included a chapter on "The Hebrews," in which Herder covers the origins of the Jewish tribe in Palestine—contrasting Manetho's account with the Old Testament. Upon their defeat by Rome and subsequent dispersion,

[21] In Poliakov (1965: 512).
[22] In Poliakov (1965: 180).

such an influence of the Jews upon the human race commenced, as could hardly have been conceived from a land
of such small extent; since these people had never distinguished themselves, in the whole course of their history, as
skilled in war or politics, and still less as inventors in the
arts and sciences (1968: 140).

Herder then comments on "the intolerant spirit of the Jewish religion,"
citing its more notable characteristics as "pride, superstition, and antipa-
thy to other nations." Upon reaching Europe, "this widely diffused republic of cunning usurers" managed to dominate finance and commerce,
though their gains were earned at the expense of workers of their host
nations. In summary,

[this] people of God...have been for thousands of years,
nay almost from their beginning, parasitical plants on the
trunks of other nations; a race of cunning brokers, almost
throughout the whole world... (144)

This is striking in his use of the term 'parasite'—apparently the first in
history, as applied to the Jews. As many previous commentators had observed, Jews have produced no people of creative genius and contributed
virtually nothing to culture or society, and yet, through their interest-
bearing loans, are able to acquire vast wealth. This wealth is produced
from 'nothing,' that is, through no productive work. Worse, it is wealth
taken directly from the pockets of the native people who are their hosts.
We can well understand the 'parasite' imagery.

A decade later, and the situation was no better. Herder wrote: "A
ministry in which the Jew is supreme..., a department or commissariat in
which Jews do the principal business...are Pontine marshes that cannot
be drained".[23] The strongest measures are called for, and there must be
no sympathy; "[we] dare not be influenced by general humane principles." Evidently, for Herder, no action was too harsh.

By the 1820s even the illustrious Wolfgang von Goethe joined the
critics. As we read in Chamberlain (1899: 346):

---

[23] In Chamberlain (1899: 345).

> [Goethe said,] "How should we let the Jews share in our
> highest culture, when they deny its origin and source?"
> And he became "violently enraged" when the law of 1823
> permitted marriage between Jews and Germans, prophesy-
> ing the "worst and most frightful consequences," particular-
> ly the "undermining of all moral feelings" and declaring
> that the bribery of the "all-powerful Rothschild" must be
> the cause of this "folly."

Enter Schopenhauer

It was around this time that renowned philosopher Arthur Schopenhauer
entered the fray. His masterpiece *World as Will and Idea* (1819) offered
a handful of passing comments on Judaism, mostly neutral observations
of history and religion. But in a passage on the development of the arts,
he briefly turns to "the history of a small, isolated, capricious, hierar-
chical (i.e. ruled by false notions), obscure people, like the Jews, despised by the great contemporary nations of the East and of the West"
(1969: 232). "It is to be regarded generally as a great misfortune," he
adds, "that the people whose former culture was to serve mainly as the
basis of our own were not, say, the Indians or the Greeks, or even the
Romans, but just these Jews."

For the next three decades, Schopenhauer said little about them, but
he returned to the topic, in a very pointed manner, in his last major work
Parerga and Paralipomena (1851). Volume One of the book begins with
a sketch of the history of idealism, and the limitations of that metaphysical view. The classic idealists are closely allied with Judeo-Christian theology, and thus "are all marred by that Jewish theism which is impervi-
ous to any investigation, dead to all research, and thus actually appears as
a fixed idea" (1974: 15). But the subsequent essay, on the history of philosophy, brings the occasion for an extended diversion on the subject:

> The real religion of the Jews, as presented and taught in
> Genesis and all the historical books up to the end of Chron-
> icles, is the crudest of all religions because it is the only one
> that has absolutely no doctrine of immortality, not even a
> trace thereof. … The contempt in which the Jews were al-

ways held by contemporary peoples may have been due in great measure to the poor character of their religion. ...

Now this wretched religion of the Jews does not [offer any conception of an afterlife], in fact it does not even attempt it. It is, therefore, the crudest and poorest of all religions and consists merely in an absurd and revolting theism. ... While all other religions endeavor to explain to the people by symbols and parables the metaphysical significance of life, the religion of the Jews is entirely immanent and furnishes nothing but a mere war-cry in the struggle with other nations. (125-126)

Volume Two elaborates on these ideas. Schopenhauer reiterates that "the religion of the Jews occupies the lowest place among the dogmas of the civilized world" (301). This sets the tone for the chapter titled "On Religion," which brings this observation:

Also we should not forget God's chosen people who, after they had stolen by Jehovah's express command the gold and silver vessels lent to them by their old and trusty friends in Egypt, now made their murderous and predatory attack on the 'Promised Land,' with the murderer Moses at their head, in order to tear away from the rightful owners, by the same Jehovah's express and constantly repeated command, showing no mercy and ruthlessly murdering and exterminating all the inhabitants, even the women and children. (357)

A footnote to the above passage adds this widely-cited remark:

Tacitus and Justinus have handed down to us the historical basis of the Exodus... We see from the two Roman authors how much the Jews were, at all times and by all nations, loathed and despised. This may be partly due to the fact that they were the only people on earth who did not credit man with any existence beyond this life and were, there-

> fore, regarded as beasts… Scum of humanity—but great master of lies [*grosse Meister im Lügen*]. [24]

The ultimate tragedy, for Schopenhauer, is that the pathetic *Judeo-Christian* culture dominated the history of Europe, rather than the better, nobler Greco-Roman: "The religion of the Greeks and Romans, those world-powers, has perished. The religion of the contemptible little Jewish race (*verachteten Judenvölkchens*), on the other hand, has been preserved…" (393).

But the Hebrew tribe is not simply defined by a religion; "[i]t is an extremely superficial and false view to regard the Jews merely as a religious sect. … On the contrary, 'Jewish Nation' is the correct expression" (263). Like Fichte and Herder, Schopenhauer was also concerned about the political consequences of integrating, and granting rights to, this Jewish Nation. The Jews were a "*gens extorris*" (refugee race), eternally uprooted, always searching for but never finding a homeland:

> Till then, it lives parasitically on other nations and their soil; but yet it is inspired with the liveliest patriotism for its own nation. This is seen in the very firm way in which Jews stick together…and no community on earth sticks so firmly together as does this. It follows that it is absurd to want to concede to them a share in the government or administration of any country. (262)

Once again we see the 'parasite' terminology that was initiated by Herder several decades earlier.

Schopenhauer, however, was more moderate than Fichte; banishment was not necessary. He was willing to grant them limited rights, *provided* they took no role in government. "Justice demands that they should enjoy with others equal civil rights; but to concede to them a share in the running of the State is absurd. They are and remain a foreign oriental race…" (264). The race could be tolerated, but the corrupt ideol-

---

[24] Payne mistranslates this sentence, interpreting the final phrase as "past master at telling lies."

ogy had to go: "We may therefore hope that one day even Europe will be purified of all Jewish mythology" (226).

Finally, Schopenhauer found much use in that little phrase *foetor Judaicus*. For him, the 'Jewish stench' represents not a literal smell but rather an intellectual odor of stale Jewish thought, arising primarily from the Old Testament. Oddly enough, he applies it most often in his critique of Jewish approaches to animal rights.[25] In the *Parerga* he criticizes Jewish philosopher Spinoza (and his view of animals) as a man who speaks "just as a Jew knows how to do, so that we others, who are accustomed to purer and worthier doctrines, are here overcome by the *foetor Judaicus*" (vol 1: 73). Of the Genesis account that God created animals for man's use, Schopenhauer exclaims, "Such stories have on me the same effect as do Jew's pitch and *foetor Judaicus*!"[26] Somewhat later he refers to "Europe, the continent that is so permeated with the *foetor Judaicus*…" (vol 2: 372). And on the same subject: "It is obviously high time that in Europe, Jewish views on nature were brought to an end… A man must be bereft of all his senses or completely chloroformed by the *foetor Judaicus* not to see [this]" (375).

Karl Marx: A Jew on the Jews

By the middle of the 19th century, the Jewish Question in Germany—that is, the debate over civil and political emancipation for the Jews—was heating up. As we have just seen, such notable figures as Fichte, Herder, Goethe, and Schopenhauer publicly opposed part or all of the equality program. One problem was that there was as yet no unified German state, only loosely aligned kingdoms and duchies; unification would come in 1870. The other issue was the nature of the Jews themselves—their religious identity, extreme reluctance to integrate, their role in financial exploitation, and their generally distasteful demeanor.

In the early 1840s, the philosopher Bruno Bauer wrote two influential anti-Jewish tracts: *Die Judenfrage* (The Jewish Question; 1842) and

---

[25] Schopenhauer was a passionate advocate for animal welfare, far ahead of his time on that count. He was the first major philosopher to incorporate them into his ethical schema.

[26] Vol. 2: 370. "Jew's pitch" is a naturally-occurring bituminous asphalt, found in ancient times around the Dead Sea and other parts of Judea.

Die Fähigkeit der heutigen Juden und Christen frei zu werden (The Capacity of Present-day Jews and Christians to become Free; 1843).[27] These have become famous in large part because they drew the attention of a 25-year-old Karl Marx, who penned a reply, *Zur Judenfrage* (On the Jewish Question), in 1843.

In the first piece, Bauer argues that the Jews are incapable of emancipation because of the exclusive nature of their religion, which places them above all others and thus creates a virtual "war against humanity." Emancipation demands universality, a recognition of the equal moral and legal standing of all men. But the Jews cannot do this—or if they did, they would cease to be Jews. Their sense of a privileged and special destiny leads to "conceit and arrogance" on their part, and accounts for past brutalities against their enemies—a kind of "rage to annihilate." In general, the Jews display a "selfish and hypochondriacal" concern for their own well-being. Consequently, they are "themselves to blame for the oppression they suffered, because they provoked it by their adherence to their law, their language, to their whole way of life." The Jews, says Bauer, "are of necessity oppressed and their suffering is incurable".[28]

Marx (1978: 40) quotes Bauer to the same effect:

> The question is whether the Jew as such, that is, the Jew who himself avows that he is constrained by his true nature to live eternally separate from men, is able to acquire and to concede to others the universal rights of man. ... As long as he remains Jewish, the limited nature which makes him a Jew must prevail over the human nature which should associate him, as a man, with other men; and it will isolate him from everyone who is not a Jew.

And it must be recalled here that Marx himself was an ethnic Jew (though raised Christian), and could thus presumably relate to these characteristics. Also worth noting is that the debate was not about some substantial minority of, say, 10% or 15% of the nation. Jews constituted not

---

[27] The first piece is translated in whole as Bauer (1958); for a partial translation, see Mendes-Flohr and Reinharz (2011). For the second of these works, see Bauer (1978).
[28] In Leopold (1999: 204).

more than 2% of any German province, and in the largest state, Prussia, they were only around 1.3% at that time.[29]

Bauer's second essay, *Die Fähigkeit*, was less pointedly critical, but did give Marx greater opportunity to comment. In the essay Bauer notes that, relatively speaking, "Christianity stands far above Judaism, the Christian far above the Jew" (1978: 147), though both are held back by their adherence to religious dogma. To gain true freedom, the Christian must only break with his religion; but the Jew has a double task: religious emancipation, and to free himself from his 'Jewish essence.' Thus, "the Jew has it harder if he wants to raise himself to freedom." But this is highly unlikely. From the standpoint of the Jew, "[his] Jewish and re-stricted essence always and at last carries away the victory over his hu-man and political duties" (136). The Jewish essence—a *racial* essence—will always trump any concerns for humanity at large. But perhaps the most serious problem was the particularly Jewish sort of relativistic, hypocritical, amoral reasoning that Bauer calls "Jewish Jesuitism":

> The Jewish Jesuitism is the naked cunning of the material egoism, common artfulness, and for all that, rude, clumsy hypocrisy, since it is concerned with entirely natural mate-rial means. It is so clumsy and repulsive, that one can only turn away from it with disgust… (139)

This way of thinking, he said, is no more than "animal cunning."

For Marx, such analysis is fine as far as it goes, but it neglects the practical details. "Let us consider," he says, "the real Jew… the *everyday* Jew" (1978: 48). Religion is secondary; Jewish essence or 'nature' is the real driver. "What is the profane basis of Judaism? *Practical* need, *self-interest*. What is the worldly cult of the Jews? *Huckstering*. What is his worldly god? *Money*." This essence is unchangeable, so if we wish to reduce the negative impact of the Jews, we must eliminate the conditions under which they thrive: "An organization of society which would abol-ish the pre-conditions and thus the very possibility of huckstering, would make the Jew impossible." It is our monetary, capitalist society that allows

---

[29] Leopold (1999: 196; note 31) reports that Jews comprised 1.2% of Prussia in 1816 and 1.4% in 1861.

Jews to flourish, and if non-Jews are dissatisfied with this then they must change this aspect of society. In a very real sense, the non-Jews are to blame for the pernicious influence of the Jews. Freeing Jews means, in reality, freeing society from the 'Jewish conditions.' Marx is pointed: "In the final analysis, the emancipation of the Jews is the emancipation of mankind from Judaism."

From their standpoint, the Jews are doing just fine, and indeed exert massively disproportionate power *without* civil rights. Marx again quotes Bauer's *Fähigkeit*:

> The Jew, who is merely tolerated in Vienna for example, determines the fate of the whole [Austrian] Empire by his financial power. The Jew, who may be entirely without rights in the smallest German state, decides the destiny of Europe. While the corporations and guilds exclude the Jew…the audacity of [Jewish] industry mocks the obstinacy of medieval institutions. … [It is] a hypocritical situation when, in theory, the Jew is deprived of political rights, while in practice he wields tremendous power and exercises on a wholesale scale the political influence which is denied him in minor matters.

Money, says Marx, has become "a world power," and since the Jew is the master of money, he thereby masters the world. (One might note, once again, how little has changed in the intervening years.) "Money is the jealous god of Israel, beside which no other god may exist." Marx closes by reiterating his main point: "The social emancipation of the Jew is the *emancipation of society from Judaism*" (52).

After that early essay, Marx wrote little on the Jews other than occasional passing comments, primarily in his letters to Friedrich Engels. His classic work *Capital* (1867) seems at times to implicitly equate them with the despised capitalists. Marx's graphic imagery evokes Jewish stereotypes, as in this infamous passage: "Capital is dead labor which, vampire-like, lives only by sucking living labor, and lives the more, the more labor it sucks" (1976: 342). Elsewhere he conjures up the old *foetor Judaicus*: "The capitalist knows that all commodities, however tattered they may look, or however badly they may smell, are in faith and in truth money, are by nature circumcised Jews…" (256). But this seems to have been the extent of his commentary.

Bauer, on the other hand, continued to write against them—and all the more urgently, as the political situation evolved. After the defeat of Napoleon in 1815, the 39 victorious German states formed a loose alliance known as the German Confederation; it was dominated by the largest state, Prussia. The next few decades saw growing public dissatisfaction and increasing agitation for a democratic constitution, both within the individual states and at the level of the Confederation. In early 1848, following the Paris rebellion, Germans in Prussia and several other states revolted. A hybrid form of a constitutional monarchy was established, but it collapsed a year later and the Confederation was restored.

Throughout this time of turmoil, Jews worked to increase their power and influence. They reasserted their signature political strategy: playing two sides against the other, and claiming victory regardless of the outcome. Thus it was that Bauer published a striking essay, in English, in the *New York Daily Tribune*, titled "The Present Position of the Jews" (1852). He begins the piece by acknowledging this very strategy: "It is a remarkable coincidence, that not only the democracy, but also the reaction, has its Jews"—that is, both the democratic revolution and the monarchical reaction had its Jewish advocates. In the revolutionary year of 1848, "there was no popular assembly in Berlin or Vienna in which one or two Jews were not the principal haranguers; there was no democratic committee in which Jews did not conduct the counsels or draft the resolutions." Clearly they hoped to gain power and civil rights through a democratic revolution, as they had with Disraeli in England. But having failed in Germany, the Jews quickly switched allegiance to the old monarchies, and in the chaos of the day, consolidated their influence. Only a few years prior, Bauer writes, the German governments actively sought to separate and ghettoize the Jews; "and now the Jews sit in the cabinets of monarchs, Jews are invited by Kings to lay before them the results of their reflection and of their philosophical inquiries."

Bauer asks, "How then are we to interpret these facts?" It is a story dating back to the Roman Empire, when the Jews "were intimately connected with the heathen [commoners] in social relations" while "at the same time they also had intimate relations with the Imperial Court…they crowded around Augustus, Tiberius, and Caligula, and succeeded in gaining their favor." Their ultimate goal was always something like democracy, a system that would give all Jews full rights and full economic privilege—and thus maximum influence and power. Rome collapsed because

> creative powers of antiquity were paralyzed, everything was brought to a dead level, the whole world had become a mass of individuals possessing equal rights… The leveling tendency of the Jews, so hostile to historical distinctions and forms, had found a congenial atmosphere for its development.

The same process was now occurring in Germany. "[Only] ten years ago, the present victory of Judaism would have been a pure impossibility." Jews capitalized on both the new constitutional democracies and the older monarchies: "Thus has the day dawned on democratic *and* reactionary Judaism." And yet Bauer was optimistic; Jews on both fronts "deceive" themselves. The democratic ones fail to realize that ancient distinctions between peoples cannot be leveled, and that "new forces" are building from below. The monarchies, on the other hand, are based in an aristocracy that is fundamentally opposed to the oriental foreigner. For the influential Jews, "everything is a lifeless calculation," which in time can only "open the eyes of the people to the difference between themselves and these [Jewish] leaders. The people begin to feel that these men have no heart for their sufferings or their joys." In short, "the people feel the total difference of race"—a difference that must inevitably reassert itself. (Jews as a distinct 'race,' as we recall, is an ancient complaint.)

But it would take longer than Bauer anticipated. German unification in 1870 brought full emancipation in all states—a process that recurred throughout much of Europe. The formation of the Austro-Hungarian Empire in 1867 began a new "liberal era" there, and, in the words of Jerry Muller (2002: 348), "[n]o group had benefited more from the liberal era than the Jews." Their rapid success was astonishing:

> By the end of the empire [in 1918], between a quarter and a third of students at the University of Vienna were Jewish. Jews dominated the liberal professions of medicine and law. They owned many of the major Austrian banks as well

as the most important newspaper in the country, the *Neue Freie Presse*.

Albert Lindemann quotes a German-Jewish writer who lived in Vienna around 1900: "[A]ll public life was dominated by Jews. The banks, the press, the theater, literature, social organizations, all lay in the hands of the Jews…"[30] All this was made possible by "liberal principles of equality"; and hence one can well understand how it is that, in the present day, such principles are proclaimed as the highest accomplishments of mankind.

In Germany, Jews quickly took up dominant positions in finance and commerce after unification, and they became closely associated with free-market capitalism and the stock exchange. "Many highly visible Jews made fortunes in dubious ways… Those Jewish newly rich in Germany…were widely regarded as especially offensive… [T]hey were unusually ruthless in their quest for monetary gain." In 1874 a popular liberal magazine reported that "90% of brokers and stock promoters in the capital [Berlin] were Jews"—"which," admits Lindemann, "may have been true" (119-120).

Toward the Turn of the Century

Such circumstances led to another wave of anti-Jewish critiques. In 1879 an influential but today little-known work appeared, *The Victory of Jewry over Germandom*, written by the journalist Wilhelm Marr.[31] In this short piece, he offers a "resigned pessimism": Germany and indeed much of the civilized world have been conquered by the Jews. Marr calls for "an open and honest admission that Israel has become a world power of the very first rank. … Without a shred of irony, I publicly proclaim the world-historical triumph of Jewry, the news of a lost battle, the victory of

---

[30] Lindemann (1997: 189). A similar situation developed in Hungary. "By the turn of the century, Jews not only dominated Hungarian finance and commerce, but were highly visible in the free professions as well, comprising just under half of Hungary's doctors, lawyers, and journalists… With over 200,000 Jewish inhabitants, Budapest had the largest Jewish community in Europe after Warsaw" (Muller, 260).

[31] The full essay can be found in Dalton (2022).

the enemy…"[32] Traditional hatred toward the Jews is based "first, in their aversion to honest labor; second, in their legally prescribed enmity toward all non-Jews." The Germans were unable to form a cohesive state and thus unable to repel the invaders:

> The slick, cunning, elastic Jews wormed their way into this confused, clumsy Germanic element. The Jews were well-suited by their purely realistic intelligence—their slyness—to look down upon Germandom, and to subdue the monarchical, knightly, lumbering German by enabling him in his vices.

The outlook is grim—"We Germans will become their slaves"—and the circumstances quite remarkable: "without striking a blow, in fact, politically persecuted through the centuries, Jewry today has become the socio-political dictator of Germany." For Marr this was a battle of cultures, and the superior culture won—it is as simple as that. And not only in Germany but all of Europe, which is doomed to suffer the same fate within one and a half centuries: "the last brief hour for condemned Europe will strike in 150 years at the most…"—which would take us to the year 2030. An inexorable process has begun, and now "it is too late. We have been so thoroughly submerged in Judaism, that all of modern society would have to be put in question, if we wanted to forcefully emerge again." Like Marx, Marr ultimately blames his fellow countrymen:

> *You* elect the alien master to your parliaments. *You* make them legislators and judges. *You* make them dictators of the state finance system. *You* deliver up your press to them… What do you expect after all this?

Marr concludes the piece—"*To Semitism belongs world mastery!*" "Let us reconcile ourselves to the inevitable since we are unable to alter it. Its name is: *Finis Germaniae*".[33]

---

[32] In Levy (1991: 77). Levy has a nearly complete translation.
[33] In Levy (1991: 78-92).

The composer Richard Wagner promoted virtually the same view-point. As early as 1850, not long after Bauer and Marx wrote their critiques, Wagner observed that the debate over Jewish emancipation was all but irrelevant; "we see ourselves rather in the position of fighting for emancipation *from* the Jews. The Jew is in fact, in the current state of this world, already more than emancipated. *He rules*, and he will continue to rule as long as money remains the power [in society]".[34] "Judaism," he adds, "is the bad conscience of our modern civilization".[35] Some of Wagner's writings, particularly *Jewry in Music* just cited, received an angry response from the European press. His explanation: "The unheard-of hostility that I have met with in the newspapers of Europe since [that work] can be understood only by taking into account, bearing in mind that all European newspapers are almost exclusively controlled by Jews…"[36]

If there was any doubt in this, Wagner surely felt vindicated just a few years later. Writing in a local newspaper in 1878, he quoted from a recent pamphlet by an unnamed German Jew, who said:

> The modern world must triumph because it is incomparably better-armed than the old, orthodox world. … German Jewry works so energetically, so colossally, so untiringly …that the greatest part of Christendom is being led, consciously or unconsciously, by modern Jewry. With few exceptions, there is no newspaper or piece of literature which is not directly or indirectly presided over by Jews.[37]

Wagner's retort: "How true!"

Three years after that, and not long after the release of Marr's work, Wagner was contemplating the virtual takeover of a once-noble German culture. In an 1881 letter to King Ludwig II of Bavaria, he said:

> I regard the Jewish race as the born enemy of pure humanity and everything that is noble in it; it is certain that we Germans will go under before them, and perhaps I am the last

---

[34] In Rather (1990: 163). For the full essay, see Dalton (2022).
[35] In ibid., 172.
[36] In ibid., 177. From Wagner's autobiography *Mein Leben* (vol. 2), 1872.
[37] In Levy (1991: 51).

German who knows how to stand up as an art-loving man
against the Judaism that is already getting control of everything.[38]

Shortly thereafter he remarked, "[I]f our culture is collapsing, there's no
harm in that; but if it collapses through *the Jews*, that's a disgrace".[39]

Also in 1881, Wagner published a short essay titled "Know Thyself"
in a Bayreuth newspaper, again criticizing the negative effects of Jews on
German society. He wrote:

> The Jew, on the other hand, is the most astonishing exam-
> ple of race consistency ever produced by world history. ...
> Even racial mixing fails to harm him; he mixes male or fe-
> male with the most foreign of races, and a Jew always
> comes to light.
>
> He has not the slightest contact with the religion of any
> civilized nation, for in truth he has no religion at all, but only
> the faith in certain promises of his God, which in no sense
> extend to a life beyond this temporal life, as in every true
> religion. ...
>
> Thus the Jew has neither to think nor ponder, nor even
> to calculate, because the hardest calculation lies in his in-
> stincts which, closed to any ideality, are perfectly finished
> in advance. A wonderful, incomparable phenomenon: *the
> plastic demon of decay of humanity*, in triumphant security
> —and German citizens as well, of a Mosaic denomination,
> the darling of liberal princes and guarantor of our imperial
> unity. (1881, vol. 6, pp. 264-274; italics added)

This passage, and in particular the italicized phrase above, caught the eye
of Joseph Goebbels, who often referred to the Jews as "plastic demons of
decay" in both his diary and speeches.

At about this same time, the economist and philosopher Eugen
Dühring published what Jacob Katz (1980: 265) called "a vitriolic and

---

[38] In Poliakov (1965: 447).
[39] In ibid., 443.

acerbic frontal attack on Jews." Titled *The Jewish Question as a Question of Race, Morals, and Culture* (1881), the essay was a learned and scientific piece, arguing that, in Katz's words, the Jews "were a unique human species with marked physical and moral characteristics"—all of which were negative. Despite his bias, Katz was compelled to admit that Dühring was "a remarkable scholar" with "a high degree of intelligence," and that his pamphlet "revealed a great measure of analytical acumen." Dühring's work captured the critical attention of a number of scholars of the day, most notably Engels and Nietzsche.

Nietzsche

Friedrich Nietzsche, of course, was himself one of the more notorious—albeit ambiguous—critics of Jews and Judaism. As early as 1869, at age 25, he was complaining in letters to Richard Wagner of "philosophical nonsense and pushy Jewry" as a cause of social degradation.[40] Later, as he began to produce full works, nearly every one included relevant comments. For example, in his early work *Human, All-Too Human* (1878) he observed in passing that "the youthful Jew of the stock exchange is the most repugnant invention of the whole human race" (sec. 475).

But it is his book *Daybreak* (1881) that inaugurates his stronger critique. Here we find him remarking that the Jews were capable of "the coldest self-possession, [and of] the subtlest outwitting and exploitation of chance and misfortune," and furthermore that "their souls have never known chivalrous noble sentiments nor their bodies handsome armor" (sec. 205). Later, in a short but seminal passage, Nietzsche observes the following: "The command 'love your enemies' had to be invented by the Jews, the best haters there have ever been" (sec. 377). He refers, of course, to the New Testament, especially passages such as Matthew (5:44) and Luke (6:27), in which Jesus proclaims this purported virtue. On Nietzsche's view, the Jesus of the New Testament was largely an "invention" of Paul, who utilized the words and ideas of a mortal Jewish rabbi to initiate a hate-filled revenge plot against the occupying Roman Empire. Only a burning hatred toward Rome could spark the creation of

---

[40] In German: *philosophischen Unfug und vordringliches Judenthum*. Letter dated 22 May (BVN-1869,4).

a 'religion of love.' Paul was thus the quintessential Jew, turning a profound hatred into something creative and vengeful. Jews, as the ultimate misanthropes, thus become the "best" haters in human history. The same idea recurs, parenthetically, in *The Gay Science* (1882), in which Nietzsche sarcastically notes that the Jews are indeed 'chosen' people, precisely because "they had a *more profound contempt* for the human being in themselves than any other people" (sec. 136).

He was more specific in a personal notebook entry of 1885. "The dangers of the Jewish soul," he wrote, include the fact, firstly, that "they try to gain a foothold in a parasitic manner." Secondly, "they know how to 'adapt' themselves, as the scientists say." Jews have become "born actors, like the octopi of Theognis, who take on the color of the rock they stick to".[41] As a result, "even the most honorable Jewish money-manager cannot resist reaching out his fingers, cold-bloodedly, for petty and fraudulent gains".[42] Nietzsche thus expresses concern about the Jewish tendency to dissembling and falsehood; what are actors, after all, but professional liars? On his view, the Jew is a chameleon-like parasite, a multi-armed octopus, one who misses no opportunity for ill-gotten gains.

By 1886 Nietzsche saw that Jewry was on the verge of dominating European culture: "That the Jews, if they wanted it...could even now have preponderance, indeed quite literally mastery over Europe, that is certain" (*Beyond Good and Evil*, sec. 251). More importantly, he was now ready to lay out details of his account of a degrading, Jewish-inspired Christian "slave morality" that ultimately would defeat the virtuous Greco-Roman "master morality":

> The Jews have brought off that miraculous feat of an inversion of values, thanks to which life on earth has acquired a novel and dangerous attraction for a couple of millennia. ...
> Their prophets...were the first to use the word 'world' as a term of contempt. This inversion of values...constitutes the

---

[41] Theognis was an ancient Greek poet who lived circa 550 BC, who remarked on the octopus' (the *polyp*, in German) ability to change its color to match its surroundings. Interestingly, Hitler also referred to the Jews as "*polyps*" or octopi; see *Mein Kampf*, vol. 2 (13.11).

[42] NF-1885,36[43].

significance of the Jewish people: they mark the beginning of the slave rebellion in morals. (sec. 195)

The "inversion"—the replacement of noble Roman values by a low and degrading Christian morality—was a remarkable accomplishment, and a veritable guidebook for any future overturning of morals.

In 1887, Nietzsche wrote a supplemental chapter to his earlier *Gay Science*. Here he comments, sarcastically and negatively, on the Jewish proclivity for shiftiness, changeability, and deception:

> As for the *Jews*, the people who possess the art of adaptability par excellence, [my line of argument] suggests immediately that one might see them virtually as a world-historical arrangement for the production of actors, a veritable breeding ground for actors. And it really is time to ask: What good actor today is *not*—a Jew? The Jew as a born *Litterat* ['man of letters'], as the true master of the European press, also exercises his power by virtue of his theatrical gifts; for the man of letters is essentially an actor: he plays the 'expert,' the 'specialist.' (sec. 361)

More consequential were a series of observations in his major work *On the Genealogy of Morals* (1887). Here, Jews and their morality come in for severe criticism—not because of their ability to succeed, but because of *what they inherently are*:

> You will have already guessed how easily the *priestly* [i.e. Jewish] way of evaluating can split from the knightly-aristocratic, and then continue to develop into its opposite. ... The knightly-aristocratic judgments of value have as their basic assumption a powerful physicality, a blooming, rich, even overflowing health, together with those things required to maintain these qualities—war, adventure, hunting, dancing, war games, and, in general, everything which involves strong, free, happy action.... As is well known, priests are the *most evil of enemies*—but why? Because they are the most powerless. From their powerlessness,

their hate grows among them into something huge and terrifying, to the most spiritual and most poisonous manifestations. The truly great haters in world history have always been priests...

Let us briefly consider the greatest example. Everything on earth which has been done against "the noble," "the powerful," "the masters," "the rulers" is not worth mentioning in comparison with what *the Jews* have done against them: the Jews, that priestly people, who knew how to get final satisfaction from their enemies and conquerors through a radical transformation of their values, that is, through an act of the *most spiritual revenge*. This was appropriate only to a priestly people with the most deeply repressed priestly desire for revenge. In opposition to the aristocratic value equations (*good = noble = powerful = beautiful = fortunate = loved by god*), the Jews, with an awe-inspiring consistency, dared to reverse things and to hang on to that with the teeth of the most profound hatred (the hatred of the powerless), that is, to "only those who suffer are good; the poor, the powerless, the low are the only good people; the suffering, those in need, the sick, the ugly are also the only pious people; only they are blessed by God; for them alone there is salvation..."

In connection with that huge and immeasurably disastrous initiative which the Jews launched with this most fundamental of all declarations of war, I recall the sentence I wrote at another time—namely, that with the Jews *the slave revolt in morality* begins... (I, sec. 7)

"What is certain," he adds, is that under the sign of Christianity, "Israel, with its vengefulness and revaluation of all values, has hitherto triumphed again and again over all other ideals, over all *nobler* ideals." He sums up the situation concisely:

The two *opposing* values "good and bad," "good and evil" have fought a fearful battle on earth for thousands of years. ... The symbol of this battle, written in a script which has remained legible through all human history up to the pre-

sent, is called "Rome against Judea, Judea against Rome."
To this point there has been no greater event than *this* war,
this posing of a question, *this* contradiction between deadly
enemies. Rome felt that the Jew was like something contrary to nature itself, its monstrous polar opposite, as it were.
In Rome the Jew was considered "*guilty* of hatred against
the entire human race".[43] And that view was correct, to the
extent that we are right to link the health and the future of
the human race to the unconditional rule of aristocratic values, the Roman values. (I, sec. 16)

Then in a notebook entry of the same year, Nietzsche again addresses
Jewish duplicity. If one thing is certain, he says, it's that the Jews are, in
some sense, deeply untrustworthy:

People of the basest origin, in part rabble, outcasts not only
from good but also from respectable society, raised away
from even the smell of culture, without discipline, without
knowledge, without the remotest suspicion that there is
such a thing as conscience in spiritual matters; simply—
Jews: with an instinctive ability to create an advantage, a
means of seduction out of every superstitious supposi-
tion... When Jews step forward as innocence itself, then
the danger is great. (*Will to Power*, sec. 199)

And in truth, they have never moved beyond their historical role as sub-
verter of society and culture. As Nietzsche writes in one of his final
works, *Antichrist* (1888):

[T]he Jews are the *most catastrophic* people of world history
... The Jewish nation...took the side of all *decadence* instincts...because it divined in them a power by means of
which one can prevail against 'the world.' The Jews...have
a life-interest in making mankind *sick*, and in inverting the

---

[43] Nietzsche quotes Tacitus here; recall discussion in Chapter Two.

concepts of 'good' and 'evil,' 'true' and 'false' in a mortal-
ly dangerous and world-maligning sense. (sec. 24)

The following section expounds on the Jewish priests and their "miracle of falsification" that resulted in the Bible. The priest "is a parasitical type of man, thriving only at the expense of all healthy forms of life." The priest inserts himself at all major life-events—birth, death, marriage—only to poison them: "the holy parasite appears in order to denature them." "In short," adds Nietzsche, "everything that contains its value *in itself* is made altogether valueless, *anti*-valuable, by the parasitism of the priest."

In the hands of the Jewish priests—Paul above all—Christianity becomes radically falsified: a lie perpetrated against the pagan masses in order to propagate a lowly 'slave morality,' thus undermining the local base of the Roman Empire:

> In Christianity, all of Judaism, a several-century-old Jewish preparatory training and technique of the most serious kind, attains its ultimate mastery as the art of lying in a holy manner. The Christian, the *ultima ratio* of the lie, is the Jew once more—even *three times* a Jew. (sec. 44)

Paul and his fellow Jews sought to destroy the power of Rome through a pernicious, manifestly false, life-destroying ideology. Christians who embrace this ideology subconsciously undermine the Empire. It is in this sense that Nietzsche can write that "the Christian is nothing more than an anarchical Jew."

The same work includes two passing references to the ancient *foetor Judaicus*. At the beginning of section 46, Nietzsche compares the original (Jewish) Christians with present-day Polish Jews; "they both do not smell good." And in section 56 he dismisses the Jewish origins of Christianity as "an ill-smelling Judaine of rabbinism and superstition".[44]

Finally, a late letter of 31 May 1888 to his friend Heinrich Köselitz, in which Nietzsche compares the Jews to the Hindu 'chandalas'—the untouchables:

---

[44] 'Judaine' is a coined word referring to Judaism conceived as a poison.

> The Jews appear to be a chandala race that learned from their masters the principles according to which a priestly caste becomes master and a people is organized… Medieval organization seems like a strange and halting attempt to regain the notions upon which the ancient Indian-Aryan society rested—but with pessimistic values that have their origin in the soil of race-decadence. — The Jews appear to be merely 'mediators'—they invented nothing. (BVN-1888,1041)

That final phrase recalls ancient complaints about the Jews contributing nothing new or creative to society.

CHAPTER 6
INTO THE 20TH CENTURY

> One might well ask, Why are there any Jews in the
> world order? That would be exactly like asking,
> Why are there potato bugs? Nature is dominated by
> the law of struggle. There will always be parasites.
>
> — J. Goebbels (2024: 205)[1]

By the end of the 1800s, the extent of Jewish wealth and power was becoming apparent to all. In 1885 French journalist Edouard Drumont wrote a large and relatively influential book titled *Jewish France*. In it he made the shocking claim that "Jews possess half of the capital in the world".[2] Focusing on France, he remarks that the total wealth of that nation is around 150 billion francs, "of which the Jews possess at least 80 billion"—slightly more than half.[3]

Incredibly, this estimate may not be far from the mark. In the US today, Jews comprise at least five of the 10 richest Americans, and at least 27 of the richest 50—with a combined wealth exceeding $650 billion. If this proportion holds up throughout the wealth hierarchy—and there is little reason to think that it doesn't—then Jews may well control around half of the total personal wealth of the United States, which is presently estimated at $170 trillion. An astonishing situation, to be sure.

Just before the turn of the century, a transplanted Englishman named Houston Chamberlain took up permanent residence in Germany and wrote vigorously in its defense. In 1899 he published a seminal book, *Foundations of the 19th Century*—a work extolling German nationalism and cultural and racial superiority. It would profoundly influence intellec-

---

[1] Diary entry for 13 May 1943.
[2] In Mendes-Flohr and Reinharz (2011: 315).
[3] Drumont adds that "Jewish wealth…is essentially parasitic and usurious," being the result of "speculation and fraud."

tuals throughout Europe, most notably the young founders of the National Socialist party: Hitler, Joseph Goebbels, and Alfred Rosenberg.

Chamberlain opens his book with a look at historical principles:

> If we contemplate the outward history of the people of Israel, it certainly offers at the first glance little that is attractive; ... all the meanness of which men are capable seems concentrated in this one small nation; ... the grinning mask of vice stares at us from out of their history in unveiled nakedness... (1968: 10)

Later he notes that "we live today in a 'Jewish age'" (329)—which, for Europeans, is a profoundly *foreign* age. "[T]his alien people, everlastingly alien, because...it is indissolubly bound to an alien law that is hostile to all other peoples—this alien people has become...a disproportionately important and, in many spheres, actually dominant constituent of our life." A century earlier, the philosopher Herder condemned those who became "willing slaves of Jewish usury"; but today, says Chamberlain, "he could say the same of by far the greatest part of the civilized world. ... [P]ractically all branches of our life have become more or less willing slaves of the Jews..."

It is foolish to speak only of a Jewish religion. In reality it is a *nation*, a single people:

> The Jewish nomocracy (that is, rule of the law) unites the Jews, no matter how scattered they may be over all the lands of the world, into a firm, uniform and absolutely political organism, in which community of blood testifies to a common past and gives a guarantee for a common future. ... This national idea culminates in the unshakable confidence in the universal empire of the Jews... (334)

Ultimate blame for the Jewish usurpation of Europe belongs not to them, but to the ruling Gentile elite who knowingly compromised themselves for the sake of money. Responsibility lies with "those Europeans who have always, from the basest motives, encouraged, protected, and fostered the disintegrating activity of the Jews—and these are primarily the

Princes and the nobility…: the Princes because they need money for their wars, the nobility because they live extravagantly" (347). And yet, even this Jewish menace will meet its end, suggests Chamberlain. "[O]f a surety he will pass away like all that has grown" (353).

This brings us to the National Socialist era and Hitler's rule. Obviously there is much more to say than can fit into one book, but it is worth mentioning a few remarks by the most prominent party members—starting with Hitler. Born in a small Austrian town in 1889, he moved to Vienna at age 18 to study art, and was confronted with the overpowering Jewish presence there—recall the quotes by Muller and Lindemann above. A decorated soldier in World War I, he came to detest the onerous settlement inflicted upon a defeated Germany. In 1919, at the age of 30, Hitler made his first entry into politics, joining the German Workers' Party (DAP). It was at this time that he was asked for his position on the Jews. He responded with a letter to one Adolf Gemlich, in a document commonly known as Hitler's 'first letter on the Jews.' It reads in part:

> If the threat with which Jewry faces our people has given rise to undeniable hostility on the part of a large section of our people, the cause of this hostility must be sought in the clear recognition that Jewry as such is deliberately or unwittingly having a pernicious effect on our nation, but mostly in personal intercourse, in the poor impression the Jew makes as an individual. As a result, antisemitism far too readily assumes a purely emotional character. But this is not the correct response. Antisemitism as a political movement may not and cannot be molded by emotional factors but only by recognition of the facts.
>
> To begin with, the Jews are unquestionably a race, not a religious community. … Through inbreeding for thousands of years, often in very small circles, the Jew has been able to preserve his race and his racial characteristics much more successfully than most of the numerous people among whom he has lived. As a result, there lives amongst us a non-German, alien race, unwilling and indeed unable to shed its racial characteristics, its particular feelings, thoughts and ambitions and nevertheless enjoying the same

political rights as we ourselves do. And since even the Jew's feelings are limited to the purely material realm, his thoughts and ambitions are bound to be so even more strongly. Their dance around the golden calf becomes a ruthless struggle for all the possessions that we feel deep down are not the highest and not the only ones worth striving for on this earth. …

All this results in that mental attitude and that quest for money and the power to protect it which allow the Jew to become so unscrupulous in his choice of means, so merciless in their use of his own ends. … His power is the power of the money, which multiplies in his hands effortlessly and endlessly through interest, and with which he imposes a yoke upon the nation that is the more pernicious in that its glitter disguises its ultimately tragic consequences. Everything that makes the people strive for higher goals, be it religion, socialism, or democracy, is to the Jew merely a means to an end, the way to satisfy his greed and thirst for power. The result of his works is racial tuberculosis of the nation. …

Rational antisemitism…must lead to a systematic and legal struggle against, and eradication of, the privileges the Jews enjoy over the other foreigners living among us (Alien Laws). Its final objective, however, must be the total removal of all Jews from our midst.[4]

The letter is striking for its relatively tempered and rational demeanor, its consistency with previous critiques, and its uncompromising attitude. The reference to tuberculosis recalls the ancient biological imagery of the Romans, as discussed previously; it was clearly no invention of Hitler's. Also noteworthy is the final line, which indicates a desire to cleanse Germany of the Jews rather than to directly punish or kill them. This in fact was a consistent stance by Hitler even throughout the war years, where even his harshest language—using terms such as *Vernichtung* and *Ausrotten*—referred to evacuation and expulsion, not mass murder.

---

[4] For the full letter, see Dalton (2022).

The majority of Hitler's recorded statements on the Jews come from two sources: his speeches and *Mein Kampf.* Of the dozens of speeches he gave over 23 years, most contained at least passing mention of the *Juden-frage*—which had now become not a matter of emancipation of the Jews, as it originally was, but of how to release German society from their grip. As important as they are, speeches are primarily rhetorical devices de-signed to sway opinion, inflame passions, or impart certain messages or impressions. They are less useful as a measure of one's considered opin-ion. *Mein Kampf* is thus our best source, and indeed the book is filled with scathing but insightful comments on the Jews. Nearly all of the 27 chapters, over two volumes, contain multiple references.[5] A representa-tive passage comes from the end of chapter 4, volume 1 (section 4.12):

> The state is a community of living beings who have kin-dred physical and spiritual natures. It is organized for the purpose of assuring the preservation of their own kind, and to help towards fulfilling those ends assigned by Provi-dence. … People who can sneak their way into the human body politic and, like parasites, make others work for them, can form a state without possessing any specific territory. This is chiefly applicable to that parasitic nation which, to-day more than ever, preys upon the honest portion of man-kind: the Jews.
>
> The Jewish State has never been delimited in space. It has been spread all over the world, without any borders whatsoever, and has always been constituted by only one race. That's why the Jews have always formed a State within the State. One of the most ingenious tricks ever de-vised has been to make this state sail under the flag of 'reli-gion,' thus assuring it of the religious tolerance that Aryans are always ready to grant. But the Mosaic religion is really nothing else than the doctrine of the preservation of the Jewish race. It therefore takes in all spheres of sociological,

---

[5] Especially heavy emphasis appears in chapters 2 and 11 of volume 1, and chapters 10 and 13 of volume 2.

political, and economic knowledge that have any bearing on this function. (Hitler 2022: 173-174)

Not mindless ranting, but a fairly reasoned and erudite assessment, particularly from a man with no formal academic training. And then consider this passage on Marx from volume 2:

> International Marxism is nothing but the application, by the Jew Karl Marx, of a pre-existing worldview to a definite profession of political faith. Without the foundation of this widely-diffused infection, the amazing success of this doctrine would have been impossible. In reality, Karl Marx was the one among millions who, in a slowly decomposing world, used his keen insight to detect the essential poisons; he then extracted and concentrated them, with the skill of a wizard, into a solution that would bring about the rapid destruction of the independent nations of this earth. And all this was done in the service of his race.
>
> Marxist doctrine is the concentrated extract of the mentality that underlies the present generally-accepted worldview. For this reason alone, it's out of the question, and even ridiculous, to think that our so-called bourgeois world can offer any effective resistance. This bourgeois world is infected with all those same poisons, and its general worldview differs from Marxism only in degree and in the person who holds it. The bourgeois world is Marxist, but believes in the possibility of rule by a certain group of people (the bourgeoisie), while Marxism itself systematically aims at delivering the world into the hands of the Jews. (vol 2, sec 1.6, p. 22)

Or this short passage on the degrading effects of Jews on culture:

> The destructive effects of the Jew's activity in other national bodies can be fundamentally ascribed to his persistent efforts at undermining the importance of personality among the host nations, and replacing it with the mass. The con-

structive principle of Aryan humanity is thus displaced by the destructive principle of the Jews. They become the 'ferment of decomposition' among nations and races and, in a broad sense, the dissolvers of human culture.[6] (vol 2, sec 4.2, pp. 83-84)

Clearly there is much more to be said on Hitler's views, but space limitations preclude further elaboration here.[7]

Intellectual Critiques by Rosenberg and Goebbels

More-learned commentary would come from the NSDAP *intelligentsia*, especially Alfred Rosenberg and Joseph Goebbels. Rosenberg earned his PhD in engineering in 1917 and joined the DAP in early 1919. Soon thereafter he began his writings on National Socialist ideology, eventually producing over 20 books and several other collections of essays and speeches. From a present-day research standpoint, one is immediately struck by the fact that English translations of his writings are very hard to find. Even the Internet has very little in English. There would seem to be a concerted effort to limit dissemination of his ideas.

The only book by a major academic publisher is *Alfred Rosenberg: Selected Writings* (1970)—a work now over 50 years old. Regarding the Jewish Question, the book contains only one chapter, "The Enemy," taken from the 1937 edition of *Die Spur des Juden im Wandel der Zeiten* (The Track of the Jews through the Ages), described by the editor as his "most comprehensive and detailed attack on Judaism" (1970: 199)—though one would hardly suspect this from the mild passages cited. Re-

---

[6] The phrase 'ferment of decomposition'—meaning an agent of social and cultural decay or disintegration—was a favorite of Hitler's. It is a paraphrase of a century-old statement by prominent German historian Theodor Mommsen. In his *History of Rome* (1854), Mommsen wrote, "Also in the ancient world, Judaism was an effective ferment of cosmopolitanism and of national decomposition..." (*Auch in der alten Welt war das Judenthum ein wirksames Ferment des Kosmopolitismus und der nationalen Decomposition...*; vol. 3, p. 550). In English translation: *The History of Rome* (1871; Dickson, trans.), vol. 4, p. 643.

[7] For a full account of Hitler's statements about the Jews, see *Hitler on the Jews* (2024; T. Dalton, ed.).

garding the Jews, Rosenberg explains that "[u]sury and fraud were the order of the day from time immemorial" (177). Throughout all of history we are confronted with this fact: "the inhabitants of all lands in which Jews are found in great numbers are surfeited with accusations of the deceitful trade of the Jews and their unbearable usury." All the wonderful moral injunctions of the Old Testament are meant for Jews alone; the Talmud in fact mandates unethical treatment for non-Jews. Rosenberg even quotes the Talmud at several points, including the following: "Canaan has taught its sons five things: to love one another, to love theft, to love dissolution, to hate thy master, and never to speak the truth" (184). Ultimately, he says, it's not only the Jews but the Germans, too, who are to blame for the present predicament:

> Left to itself, the German character would have achieved a balance. However, this was made impossible due to Jewish strength in the press, theater, trade, and sciences. We ourselves have been guilty—we should not have emancipated the Jews but, as Goethe, Fichte, and Herder vainly demanded, should have created insurmountable exceptional laws for them. One does not allow a poison to drift about unobserved, nor grant it parity with medicine; rather one keeps it within careful limits. (188-189)

And yet, English publishers have studiously avoided all of Rosenberg's other books, especially his great masterpiece *The Myth of the Twentieth Century*—second in importance only to *Mein Kampf*. For decades, the only English editions were poor efforts by renegade publishers; and only in 2021 did a professional translation finally become available.[8]

 Myth is not only a masterpiece of history and theory, it is the articulation of a complete worldview and philosophy of life. But more to the point, it contains a number of biting remarks against the Jews. The Jews have created a world mythology, a mythos, "which emanated from the Jewish parasitical dream of world domination" (2001: 273). Their "black

---

[8] This is the Clemens & Blair edition, edited by T. Dalton. The following quotations come from this edition.

magic of politics and trade" and "impulsive power to acquire gold" served as tools for attacking and draining foreign nations and cultures:

> Where any kind of wound is torn open in the body of a nation, the Jewish demon always eats itself into the infected part and, as a parasite, it exploits the weak hours of the great nations of this world. His mentality is not to fight as a hero for enlightened, constructive rule, but to make the world liable to financial interest. This is the direction of this parasite, strong of strong—not to fight, but to creep; not to serve values, but to devaluate. These things constitute his law, according to which he has moved and from which he can never escape, as long as he exists. (274)

Jewish parasitism, says Rosenberg, is a "biological fact," no different from other parasites in nature. The Jew is not a race but an *anti-race*, one that "penetrates into society through the open wounds," and then "feeding off [the people's] racial and creative strength until their decline" (275). Where other social parasites exist, they are drawn to the Jews—as when the "scum of Egypt left the land of the pharaohs along with the Hebrews." The Jewish "demon of eternal denial" promotes only a "shapeless anarchism" that serves his cause. Thus, the "world hope of the 'chosen' consists in living off all the nations as a sucking parasite. ... The ancient mythos of the chosen people bred a new type of parasitism with the aid of modern technology and the one-world civilization idea of a world grown soulless" (277-278).

   Elsewhere in the book he argues that Jews are crude materialists ("The motivating force of Judaism is always material gain"; p. 191), cultural corruptors ("the whole of Jewry made itself into the promoter of black art in all domains"; p. 253), and supreme liars ("the constant lie is the organic truth of the Jewish anti-race"; p. 427). *Myth* contains much more than Jewish critique, of course, and in fact constitutes a virtual mastercourse in National Socialist ideology. As such, it serves as an intellectual counterpart and essential supplement to Hitler's earlier *Mein Kampf*.

   For his part, Joseph Goebbels earned a PhD in history and philology in 1921, and joined the National Socialist party three years later. He immediately impressed not only Hitler but others with his learned demeanor and mental acuity. The American diplomat to Germany, Hugh Wilson, referred to Goebbels as "this man of high intelligence," and found him a stimulating conversationalist.[9] Even his enemies were impressed; a Marxist, Oswald Dutch, wrote the following in 1940:

> He is blessed with a superabundance of intellect and wit. In his particular sphere, he might be called frankly a genius. … Dr. Goebbels possesses a mind that is keen, practical, and sober; able to cope, with lightning rapidity, with any situation; unconquerable, and never at a loss. [H]e is so mentally versatile that it is almost impossible to do him justice.[10]

For over 20 years, Goebbels kept a near-daily diary, a full copy of which was only uncovered in the mid-1990s. It offers unprecedented insight into the workings of National Socialist Germany, and more to the point, of its attitudes toward the Jews. The following are only a few passages of interest.[11]

His earliest references to the *Judenfrage* date to the first year of entries (1924), but it would be some 10 years before Goebbels began to discuss serious action against the Jews. By the late 1930s, German leadership was increasingly concerned about American involvement, and about America's motivation for agitating against Germany. Roosevelt and his advisors were pinpointed as a source of the problem: "Roosevelt is our enemy. He is surrounded by Jews".[12] And then two months later: "Roosevelt speaks out ever harsher against us. He is totally in the hands of the Jews. A Jew-slave, perhaps even of Jewish ancestry".[13] Goebbels would eventually come to see America as a lost cause: "The USA has now published statistics that there are 5,000,000 religious Jews in the United States. You can really call the US a first-class Jew-state".[14]

---

[9] Wilson (1941: 191). Wilson added, "Among the leading men of the Nazi Party there is none who…is so well able to expound the Nazi doctrine, or so competent to meet the foreigner upon his own ground" (p. 292).

[10] Dutch (1940: 67).

[11] For a full account of the diary entries on Jews, see Goebbels (2024). The following quotations are taken from this book.

[12] Entry dated 17 Sep 1938.

[13] Entry dated 27 Nov 1938.

[14] Entry dated 17 Apr 1943.

Into the war years, a series of illuminating comments:

- "The Jewish problem will probably be the hardest to solve. These Jews are no longer human beings. [They are] predators equipped with a cold intellect, which must be rendered harmless".[15]

- "The Jewish Question has again become especially acute in the Reich capital. We count 70,000 Jews in Berlin at the moment, of which 30,000 are not even working; the others live as parasites off the work of the host nation. This is an intolerable situation. … I also think it necessary that the Jews be given a badge [the yellow Star of David]. They are active in public life as defeatists and mood-spoilers. It is therefore imperative that they be recognized as Jews".[16]

- "Jewry is a foreign body among civilized nations, and its activities in the past three decades has been so devastating that the people's reaction is understandable—indeed, one might say, a compulsion of nature".[17]

- "We fly early in the morning to Vilnius [Lithuania]. … Thousands [of Jews] have been shot, and even now hundreds more as well. They have now all been rounded up into their ghettos. … [O]n a short drive through the ghetto, the view is horrifying. Here the Jews squat in rows, hideous forms, not to be looked at let alone touched. … Even 10 years ago, I would not have dreamed that something like this would ever be the case. Terrible figures lurk in the streets, which I would not like to meet at night. The Jews are the lice of civilized man".[18]

- "The sufferings of the Russian people under Bolshevism are indescribable. This Jewish terrorism must be rooted out, stump and stem, from all of Europe. That is our historical task. … Jewry

---

[15] Entry dated 7 Oct 1939.
[16] Entry dated 12 Aug 1941.
[17] Entry dated 19 Aug 1941.
[18] Entry dated 2 Nov 1941.

will undoubtedly experience a catastrophe along with Bolshevism. The Führer once again expressed his opinion that he is determined to ruthlessly clean up the Jews in Europe. Here one
must not have any sentimental tendencies. The Jews deserve the
catastrophe they are experiencing today. ... We are doing an incalculable service to a humanity that has been tormented by
Jewry for millennia".[19]

The British were also heavily influenced by Jewish money, and Churchill
in particular was eager to please—a point not lost on Goebbels: "Churchill openly stands on the side of the Jews. He is a consummate servant of
the Jews".[20] Across the Atlantic, Jewish-American media was working
full time to thrust America into the war. The Germans were keeping a
close eye on the situation:

> I am given some statistics on the proportion of Jewry in
> American radio, film, and press. The percentage is truly
> frightening. Jewry controls 100% of the film business, and
> between 90 and 95% of press and radio. These facts explain
> the confused mental warfare of the other side. The Jews are
> not as clever as they would make us believe. If they are in
> danger, they become the stupidest of devils....
>   [W]herever you look, the wire-puller in the background
> is international Jewry. We will be doing humanity a great
> service if we finally remove them from public life and stick
> them in quarantine.[21]

Note the repeated emphasis on "clearing out," "removal," "quarantine,"
and so on—and no talk of mass murder, gas chambers, etc. This is not
due to selective editing; *nowhere* in Goebbels' vast diary is there mention
of such action.
    Nor was he beyond the occasional bit of dry humor. On 18 Decem-
ber 1942 he wrote, "The Jews of Jerusalem are holding noisy protests
against us. They had a day of fasting, and at the Wailing Wall, they in-

---

[19] Entry dated 15 Feb 1942.
[20] Entry dated 17 Nov 1941.
[21] Entry dated 24 Apr 1942.

voked the Old Testament Jewish curse against the Führer, Göring, Himmler, and me. So far I haven't noticed any effect…" The same entry included a comment on the unwillingness of Sweden to accept Jewish refugees: "The Swedes protest hypocritically against our treatment of the Polish Jews, but are unwilling to receive them in their country. … It would probably be a good thing if the Swedes were to admit a few thousand such Jews into their country. That would give them a practical lesson in the Jewish Question".[22]

On 18 February 1943, Goebbels gave a major public address in Berlin, formally titled "Nation Rise Up," but also known as the "Total War" speech. It included these striking words on the Jewish problem:

> The goal of Bolshevism is Jewish world revolution. They want to bring chaos to the Reich and Europe, using the resulting hopelessness and desperation to establish their international, Bolshevist-concealed capitalist tyranny. … The German nation is unwilling to bow to this danger. Behind the oncoming Soviet divisions, we see the Jewish liquidation commandos, and behind them terror, the specter of mass starvation and complete anarchy. International Jewry is the devilish ferment of decomposition that finds cynical satisfaction in plunging the world into the deepest chaos and destroying ancient cultures that it played no role in building.
>
> We also know our historic responsibility. Two thousand years of Western civilization are in danger. One cannot overestimate the danger. It is indicative that when one names it as it is, international Jewry throughout the world protests loudly. Things have gone so far in Europe that one cannot call a danger a danger, when it's caused by the Jews. …
>
> Jewry has so deeply infected the Anglo-Saxon states, both spiritually and politically, that they are no longer have the ability to see the danger. It conceals itself as Bolshevism in the Soviet Union, and as plutocratic-capitalism in the Anglo-Saxon states. The Jewish race is an expert at

---

[22] Note that Goebbels is well-disposed toward deporting Jews rather than killing them—and this at the height of the alleged extermination process.

mimicry. They put their host peoples to sleep, paralyzing their defensive abilities. Our insight into the matter led us to the early realization that cooperation between international plutocracy and international Bolshevism was not a contradiction, but rather a sign of deep commonalities. The hand of the pseudo-civilized Jewry of Western Europe shakes the hand of the Jewry of the Eastern ghettos over Germany. Europe is in deadly danger. ...

[T]he danger is immediate. The paralysis of the Western European democracies before their deadliest threat is frightening. International Jewry is doing all it can to encourage such paralysis. During our struggle for power in Germany, Jewish newspapers tried to conceal the danger, until National Socialism awakened the people. It is just the same today in other nations. Jewry once again reveals itself as the incarnation of evil, as the plastic demon of decay, and the bearer of an international culture-destroying chaos.

In mid-1943 came a lengthy diary entry on the nature of Jewry, beginning with a reflection on the *Protocols of Zion*—a document of uncertain origin, detailing a Jewish plan for world domination:

I have devoted exhaustive study to the *Protocols of Zion*. In the past the objection was always made that they were not suited to present-day propaganda. In reading them now, I find that we can use them very well. The *Protocols of Zion* are as modern today as they were when published for the first time... At noon I mentioned this to the Führer. He believed the *Protocols* were absolutely genuine....[23]

The Jewish Question, in the Führer's opinion, will play a decisive role in England.... In all the world, he said, the Jews are alike. Whether they live in a ghetto of the East or in the bankers' palaces of the City or Wall Street, they will always pursue the same aims and without previous agree-

---

[23] For a recent, detailed study of the Protocols, including commentary by National Socialists, see Dalton, ed. (2023).

ment even use the same means. One might well ask, Why are there any Jews in the world order? That would be exactly like asking, Why are there potato bugs? Nature is dominated by the law of struggle. There will always be parasites who will spur this struggle on and intensify the process of selection between the strong and the weak. The principle of struggle dominates also in human life. One must merely know the laws of this struggle to be able to face it. The intellectual does not have the natural means of resisting the Jewish peril because his instincts have been badly blunted. Because of this fact the nations with a high standard of civilization are exposed to this peril first and foremost. In nature, life always takes measures against parasites; in the life of nations that is not always the case. From this fact the Jewish peril actually stems. There is therefore no other recourse left for modern nations except to root out the Jew.

There is no hope of leading the Jews back into the fold of civilized humanity by exceptional punishments. They will forever remain Jews, just as we are forever members of the Aryan race.

The Jew was also the first to introduce the lie into politics as a weapon. Aboriginal man, the Führer believes, did not know the lie.... The higher the human being developed intellectually, the more he acquired the ability of hiding his innermost thoughts and giving expression to something different from what he really felt. The Jew, as an absolutely intellectual creature, was the first to learn this art. He can therefore be regarded not only as the carrier but even the inventor of the lie among human beings. Because of their thoroughly materialistic attitude, the English act very much like the Jews. In fact, they are the Aryans who have acquired most of the Jewish characteristics.... The nations that have been the first to see through the Jew and have been the first to fight him are going to take his place in the domination of the world.[24]

---

[24] Entry dated 13 May 1943.

And a final observation by Goebbels, from late in the war: "The Jew is really the ferment of decomposition, and the real culprit of this war. He and his race will therefore likely have to pay the highest price for this war".[25]

Such criticism came not only from the National Socialists; even the loftiest of German intelligentsia had critical comments. Consider a few remarks by Martin Heidegger, undoubtedly one of the most consequential philosophers of the 20th century. In a recent book, *Heidegger and the Myth of a Jewish World Conspiracy* (2015), Peter Trawny cites a number of interesting passages, including mention of the Jews' "empty rationality" and "calculative ability," their tendency to "'live according to the principle of race," and of the equating of "Americanism" and Bolshevism with "world Judaism" (2015: 18-19).

The hazard presented by world Jewry, according to Heidegger, was very concrete and very severe. "There truly is a dangerous international band of Jews," he said (27). And in one of the most striking phrases of age, he further referred to the Jews as "planetary master criminals of the most modern modernity," and to "the peculiar predetermination of Jewry for planetary criminality" (33).[26]

But the danger is not transparent; "World Judaism…is everywhere elusive" (30). They hide in the background, unseen, the invisible "wire-pullers" that Hitler spoke of. Even at the philosophical level, Jews pose a kind of ontological risk: "In the period of the Christian West, i.e. of metaphysics, Jewry is the principle of destruction" (73). For Heidegger, it seems, one cannot overstate the danger posed by the Jews.

---

[25] Entry dated 13 Dec 1944. Clearly, if the Jews have yet to pay "the highest price," they haven't been exterminated. Also recall the use of the phrase 'ferment of decomposition'; see note 6 above.

[26] As one witnesses the genocide in Palestine and the prominent Jewish role in the Ukraine-Russia war, not to mention various acts of mayhem conducted by the Mossad around the world, we see that Heidegger was firmly on the mark: "planetary master criminals."

CHAPTER 7
JUDAICA AMERICANA

[The Jew] is substantially a foreigner wherever he may be… You [Jews] will always be, by ways and habits and predilections, substantially strangers—foreigners—wherever you are…
——Mark Twain (1899: 535)

You can really call the US a first-class Jew-state.
——Joseph Goebbels (2024: 186)

In his 1911 book *The Jews and Modern Capitalism*, German economist Werner Sombart made this striking assertion: "For what we call Americanism is nothing else than the Jewish spirit distilled" (44). What could prompt such a claim? And in 1911 already?

From a present-day perspective, it's clear that a "Jewish spirit" does indeed dominate American culture. But so too does a spirit of critique and resistance. Historically speaking, anti-Jewish sentiment was widespread in the US, and it extended to some of its most famous writers, philosophers, and intellectuals. This fact suggests, once again, that there are certain objectionable or problematic qualities that are intrinsic to the Jewish character, and that these have become repeatedly manifest over time.

From the very beginning of the American enterprise, Jews were present and active. Sombart (1911: 41) called them the "golden thread in the tapestry…of America's economic history." He cites the year 1655 as their first recorded appearance, and notes that "it was due to them that the [American] colonies were able to maintain their existence." In the critical early years of the 1600s and 1700s, "the trade of the Jews was the source from which the economic system of the colonies drew its life-blood." Sombart gives numerous examples of influential Jews: Levi in Albany (1661); Mordecai in Alabama (1785); Schubert and Newburg in Chicago; Solomon in Lexington (1816); de Cordova, Koppore, and Castro in Texas (mid-1800s); the Seligman family in New York and San Francisco (mid-1800s). Jews were prominent owners of southern plantations, and thus complicit in slavery.[1] They were among the first businessmen to move west; "California is, for the most part, their creation."

Into the early 20th century, Sombart observes that "the Jews in America practically control a number of important branches of commerce; indeed, it is not too much to say that they monopolize them"—citing in particular gold, wheat, tobacco, cotton, and finance. And he quotes former president Grover Cleveland: "I believe that it can be safely claimed that few, if any, of those contributing nationalities have directly and indirectly been more influential in giving shape and direction to the Americanism of today [than the Jews]." All of which leads to his conclusion, cited above, that "Americanism is nothing else than the Jewish spirit distilled."

If all this is true, we should find some reaction among the American leadership—and indeed we do. George Washington evidently had concerns about Jewish influence. An 1894 book of his political maxims refers to this influence twice, but indirectly. In a section headed "Speculators in the currency," Washington is recorded as saying, "This tribe of black gentry works more effectually against us, than the enemy's arms. They are a hundred times more dangerous to our liberties, and the great cause we are engaged in" (1894: 125). The 'black gentry' would seem to refer to the Orthodox (Hassidic) Jews, who traditionally wear black clothing.[2] If this is in doubt, the following passage makes things clear:

> It is much to be lamented, that each State, long ere this, has not hunted them down, as pests to society, and the greatest enemies we have to the happiness of America. I would to God, that some one of the most atrocious in each State, was hung from a gallows, five times as high as the one prepared by Haman. No punishment, in my opinion,

---

[1] This account is detailed in the book *The Secret Relationship between Blacks and Jews* (Nation of Islam, 3 volumes, 2017-2023).

[2] It is clear that he cannot mean African-Americans: first, there were no 'gentry' among the slaves; second, if there were, they certainly were not involved in currency speculation; and third, he would undoubtedly have used the word 'Negro.'

is too great for the man who can build his greatness upon
his country's ruin. (126)

The 'gallows of Haman' can only refer to the biblical story of Esther, and
Haman's desire to hang the Jew Mordecai from 25 meters high.[3] The
two passages are dated a year apart (1778 and 1779) and we lack the context, but they seem to indicate a persistent concern.[4]

One might consider Washington's comments anomalous—except
he wasn't alone among early American presidents. Thomas Jefferson,
writing in a letter of 21 April 1803, commented on the relative merits of
various religions. On Judaism, he wrote:

Jews. Their system was Deism; that is, belief in one only
God. But their ideas of him and his attributes were degrading and injurious. Their Ethics were not only imperfect, but
often irreconcilable with the sound dictates of reason and
morality, as they respect intercourse with those around us;
and repulsive and anti-social, as respecting other nations.
They needed reformation, therefore, in an eminent degree.
(1905: 382)

---

[3] See Chapter One.

[4] Washington's comments are often found on the Internet paired with a more
explicit and more critical passage allegedly by Benjamin Franklin. However, I
have been unable to verify its authenticity. It reads in part: "I fully agree with
General Washington, that we must protect this young nation from an insidious
influence and impenetration. The menace, gentlemen, is the Jews. In whatever
country Jews have settled in any great number, they have lowered its moral
tone; depreciated its commercial integrity; have segregated themselves and
have not been assimilated; have sneered at and tried to undermine the Christian
religion upon which that nation is founded, by objecting to its restrictions;
have built up a state within the state… [T]hey are vampires, and vampires do
not live on vampires. They cannot live only among themselves. They must
subsist on Christians and other people not of their race. If you do not exclude
them from these United States, in their Constitution, in less than 200 years they
will have swarmed here in such great numbers that they will dominate and
devour the land and change our form of government, for which we Americans
have shed our blood, given our lives our substance and jeopardized our liberty."

And then consider John Quincy Adams—our sixth president, son of our second. As a young man traveling in Europe, he encountered some Jews in a synagogue in Amsterdam. He wrote in his diary that they were "all wretched creatures, for I think I never saw in my life such a set of miserable looking people, and they would steal your eyes out of your head if they possibly could".[5] Youthful impetuousness, perhaps? But some years later, around 1804, he gave a speech decrying the numerous Jews of Frankfurt, Germany: "the word 'filth' conveys an ideal of spotless purity in comparison with Jewish nastiness".[6] Even late in life, after serving as president, Adams' distaste for the Jews never diminished. A diary entry of a decade later indicates agreement with a speaker that Adams had heard earlier that day, condemning the Jews as "the worst" of the peoples of Turkey, and noting that "their hatred of all Christians is rancorous beyond conception".[7] By the 1840s Jews were running for, and winning, their first congressional seats—David Levy Yulee was the first Jewish senator (from Florida) and Lewis Levin the first representative (Pennsylvania), both in 1845. Yulee was a secessionist, and this undoubtedly encouraged Adams to refer to him in derogatory terms: the "Jew delegate from Florida," the "alien Jew," and "the squeaking Jew delegate from Florida".[8]

Secession was also on the mind of senator and future president Andrew Johnson in 1861. He is quoted referring to Yulee as "the contemptible little Jew who wants Florida to secede".[9] Upon issuing this complaint, Johnson denounced Judah Benjamin, the second Jewish senator (from Louisiana): "There's another Jew—that miserable Benjamin! He looks on a country and a government as he would on a suit of old clothes. He sold out the old one; and he would sell out the new if he could in so doing make two or three millions."

During the Civil War, as during most wars in history, Jews profited handsomely.[10] General William Sherman complained that Tennessee "swarms with dishonest Jews who will smuggle powder, pistols, percus-

---

[5] In Dinnerstein (1994: 11).
[6] In Jaher (1994: 135).
[7] In ibid., 146.
[8] In ibid., 190.
[9] In ibid., 190.
[10] Sombart (pp. 50-53) makes precisely this point.

sion caps, etc." to the enemy. Ulysses S. Grant was commander of the Department of Tennessee, and he evidently agreed. In October 1862 he wrote that "Israelites should be kept out" because they were "an intolerable nuisance." Then on December 8 Grant issued the first of two infamous orders: General Order #2, mandating that

> cotton-speculators, Jews and other Vagrants, having not honest means of support, except trading upon the miseries of their country…will leave in 24 hours or they will be sent to duty in the trenches.[11]

This was followed on December 17 by an even more sweeping decree, General Order #11:

> Jews, as a class, violating every regulation of trade established by the Treasury Department, and also Department orders, are hereby expelled from the Department [of Tennessee]. [They have 24 hours] to leave, and anyone returning after such notification, will be arrested and held in confinement until an opportunity occurs of sending them out as prisoners.[12]

The order did not stand; Lincoln issued an immediate counter-mandate, believing it unwise to banish Jews "as a class." Grant, of course, would go on to become president in 1869.

American Writers Take Notice

It was around this time that major American writers began to take note of the Hebrews, beginning with Ralph Waldo Emerson and Nathaniel Hawthorne. In his *English Traits* (1856), in the chapter on "Race," Emerson wrote, "Race is a controlling influence in the Jew, who, for two millenniums, under every climate, has preserved the same character and employments" (1929, vol 4: 47). Four years later, his *Conduct of Life*

---

[11] In Jaher (1994: 199).

[12] Both orders can also be found in *The Papers of Ulysses S. Grant*, vol 7 (pages 9 and 58, respectively).

(1860)—in the essay titled "Fate"—reflects on history: "We see how much will has been expended to extinguish the Jew, in vain" (vol 5: 16). This is because Jews are a tough and successful race, made hard by suffering: "The sufferance which is the badge of the Jew, has made him, in these days, the ruler of the rulers of the earth" (vol 5: 35).

Hawthorne's nonfiction *English Notebooks* of 1856 recalls a British dinner party with some local dignitaries—among whom was a prominent Jew and his wife. The woman was beautiful, "but I never should have thought of touching her, nor desired to touch her; for, whether owing to distinctness of race, my sense that she was a Jewess, or whatever else, I felt a sort of repugnance..." Regarding her husband, Hawthorne had this to say:

> [T]here sat the very Jew of Jews; the distilled essence of all the Jews that have been born since Jacob's time; he was Judas Iscariot; he was the Wandering Jew; he was the worst, and at the same time, the truest type of his race, and contained within himself, I have no doubt, every old prophet and every old clothesman, that ever the tribes produced; and he must have been circumcised as much as ten times over. I never beheld anything so ugly and disagreeable, and preposterous, and laughable, as the outline of his profile; it was so hideously Jewish, and so cruel, and so keen... Well; it is as hard to give an idea of this ugly Jew, as of the beautiful Jewess. ... I rejoiced exceedingly in this Shylock, this Iscariot; for the sight of him justified me in the repugnance I have always felt towards his race. (1856/1962: 321)

The trend initiated by Blake, Emerson, and Hawthorne accelerated in the several decades after the Civil War. Over the 80-year period from 1860 to 1940, more than a dozen prominent writers expressed concern about the role of Jews in Anglo-American culture. Many came to be slandered as "anti-Semites." This is notable because, in many cases, the comments were rather mild, isolated, or just simple expressions of fact. But the Jewish community takes even the barest of criticism—even a single incident—as a dagger to the heart; unless it is immediately followed by a gushing apology, the offender is thereafter permanently tarred with the Jew-hating label.

The first of this group to comment was Frederick Law Olmstead, the famous landscape architect and some-time essayist. His two-volume work *Journeys and Explorations in the Cotton Kingdom* (1861) contains several observations on the slave industry in the American South. Of the many evils he found there, one was the intrusion of Northern Jews seeking to profit from the situation:

> A swarm of Jews, within the last ten years, has settled in nearly every Southern town, many of them men of no character, opening cheap clothing and trinket shops; ruining, or driving out of business many of the old retailers, and engaging in an unlawful trade with the simple Negroes, which is found very profitable. (1861: 252)

A few decades later, Scottish author Robert Louis Stevenson traveled to the American West, and recorded his observations in the book *Across the Plains* (1892). California was developing rapidly at that time, and was in the process of transforming from a Mexican/Hispanic culture to a more strictly American one. As the economy grew, so did the Jewish presence. The effects were comparable to what Olmstead saw in the South:

> Jew storekeepers have already learned the advantage to be gained from this; they lead on the farmer into irretrievable indebtedness, and keep him ever after as their bond-slave hopelessly grinding in the mill. So the whirligig of time brings in its revenges, and except that the Jew knows better than to foreclose, you may see Americans bound in the same chains with which they themselves had formerly bound the Mexican. (1892/1906: 101)

For Stevenson, as for Olmstead, Jews were ruthless manipulators and exploiters—not quite law-breakers, but yet all too willing to take maximum advantage of those who were less clever, more naïve, or simply poor in means.

The Bard from Hannibal

Mark Twain was never known for his anti-Jewish sentiments, but he nonetheless got himself into hot water over some all-too-honest remarks. Twain lived in Austria in the late 1890s, and wrote often on the state of Viennese culture and politics. In March of 1898 he published a nonfiction essay, "Stirring times in Austria," lampooning the sorry state of the 'multicultural' Austro-Hungarian empire. Amidst the broad diversity of cultures, classes, and languages, Twain observed one common fact:

> As to the makeup of the House [of Parliament], it is this: the deputies come from all the walks of life and from all the grades of society. There are princes, counts, barons, priests, peasants, mechanics, laborers, lawyers, judges, physicians, professors, merchants, bankers, shopkeepers. They are religious men, they are earnest, sincere, devoted, and they hate the Jews. (1898: 533)

That last bit was no doubt intended as wry humor, as it had no real bearing on the issue at hand. But it was nevertheless true. Later, while recounting a particularly raucous session, he quotes deputies hurling various epithets at each other, including "You Jew!," "I would rather take my hat off to a Jew!," and "Jew-flunky! (*Judenknecht*)" The lengthy essay ends with the collapse of the Austrian government and sporadic rioting throughout the realm. "The Jews and Germans were harried and plundered, and their houses destroyed... and in all cases the Jew had to roast, no matter which side he was on" (540).

That essay drew several responses from readers, many of whom were Jews. Their outcry prompted Twain to make amends by writing a second piece, "Concerning the Jews," in late 1899. Suffice to say, it did not go as planned. He opens with excerpts from one particular letter by a Jewish lawyer expressing some half-dozen points of concern: What accounts for the unjust treatment of Jews? What can they do about it? Will the persecution ever end? and so on. Implicit in the letters was the notion that Twain was somehow insensitive to Jewish suffering, and perhaps even prejudiced against them. Twain defends himself—"I have no such prejudice"—and then proceeds to give as explicit an apology for the

Jews as he can ("His race is entitled to be called the most benevolent of all the races of men," etc.).

But Twain's inveterate honesty betrays him. He notes, for example, that "the immense wholesale business of Broadway, from the Battery to Union Square, is substantially in his hands" (1899: 529)—by way of demonstrating Jewish proficiency in business. Despite all these virtues, "the Jew has his other side":

> He has some discreditable ways, though he has not a mo-nopoly of them, because he cannot get entirely rid of vexa-tious Christian competition. We have seen that he seldom transgresses the laws against crimes of violence. Indeed, his dealings with courts are almost restricted to matters con-nected with commerce. He has a reputation for various small forms of cheating, and for practicing oppressive usury, and for burning himself out [i.e. arson] to get the insurance, and for arranging cunning contracts which leave him an ex-it but lock the other man in, and for smart evasions which find him safe and comfortable just within the strict letter of the law, when court and jury know very well that he has vi-olated the spirit of it. [Overall,] the Christian can claim no superiority over the Jew in the matter of good citizenship. Yet in all countries, from the dawn of history, the Jew has been persistently and implacably hated, and with frequency persecuted. (529-530)

Twain then recalls the story in Genesis 47 wherein Joseph the Jew, work-ing at the behest of the Pharaoh, exploits an Egyptian famine to swindle the natives out of their money, livestock, and land. "Was Joseph estab-lishing a character for his race which would survive long in Egypt? ... It is hardly to be doubted." Next, Twain recounts his boyhood days in the South, and the Jewish influence there. In the manner of Olmstead and Stevenson, he writes,

> In the cotton States, after the war, the simple and ignorant negroes made the crops for the white planter on shares. The Jew came down in force, set up shop on the plantation,

supplied all the negro's wants on credit, and at the end of
the season was proprietor of the negro's share of the present crop and of part of his share of the next one. Before
long, the whites detested the Jew, and it is doubtful if the
negro loved him.

Over time, the Russians, British, Spaniards, and Austrians had to banish
the Jews. And now the call was being heard once more, this time in
Germany:

> In Berlin, a few years ago, I read a speech which frankly
> urged the expulsion of the Jews from Germany; and the ag-
> itator's reason was as frank as his proposition. It was this:
> that eighty-five per cent of the successful lawyers of Berlin
> were Jews, and that about the same percentage of the great
> and lucrative businesses of all sorts in Germany were in the
> hands of the Jewish race! Isn't it an amazing confession?

"The Jew," adds Twain, "is a money-getter...[and] his success has made
the whole human race his enemy" (532).

And then yet once again, Twain's humor runs afoul of political correctness:

> When I read in the [encyclopedia] that the Jewish popula-
> tion of the United States was 250,000, I wrote the editor,
> and explained to him that I was personally acquainted with
> more Jews than that in my country, and that his figures
> were without a doubt a misprint for 25,000,000. ... His an-
> swer miscarried, and I never got it; but I went around talk-
> ing about the matter, and people told me they had reason to
> suspect that for business reasons many Jews whose dealings
> were mainly with the Christians did not report themselves as
> Jews in the census. It looked plausible; it looks plausible
> yet. Look at the city of New York; and look at Boston, and
> Philadelphia, and New Orleans, and Chicago, and Cincin-
> nati, and San Francisco—how your race swarms in those
> places!—and everywhere else in America, down to the

> least little village. … I am strongly of the opinion that we
> have an immense Jewish population in America. (533-534)

He then moves on to the nascent Zionist movement and the push "to gather the Jews of the world together in Palestine." "I am not objecting," says Twain, cautiously. "But if that concentration of the cunningest brains in the world was going to be made in a free country, I think it would be politic to stop it. It will not be well to let that race find out its strength." A prescient warning.

So, despite all the pogroms and persecutions throughout history, the Jew has done very well for himself:

> Among the high civilizations he seems to be very comforta-
> bly situated indeed, and to have more than his proportionate
> share of the prosperities going. It has that look in Vienna. …
> By his make and ways, he is substantially a foreigner wher-
> ever he may be, and even the angels dislike a foreigner. …
> You will always be by ways and habits and predilections
> substantially strangers—foreigners—wherever you are, and
> that will probably keep the race prejudice against you alive.
> (535)

Twain concludes with a few more inconvenient truths: "[Due to his small numbers,] properly the Jew ought hardly to be heard of; but he is heard of, has always been heard of. He is as prominent on the planet as any other people, and his commercial importance is extravagantly out of proportion to the smallness of his bulk." The little Hebrew tribe took on the world and outlasted all its enemies—Egyptians, Greeks, Romans. "The Jew saw them all, beat them all, and is now what he always was…" Indeed: "All things are mortal but the Jew; all other forces pass, but he remains. What is the secret of his immortality?" Twain closes with this question lingering in our minds; it is clear he has no answer.

Transition to the 20th Century: Henry Adams and William James

Henry Adams (b. 1838) was a historian, journalist, and novelist. He was also a member of the famous political family of Massachusetts; both his grandfather (John Quincy Adams—recall discussion above) and great grandfather (John Adams) were US presidents. Anti-Jewish themes are scattered throughout his writings. For example, his nonfiction work of 1905, *Mont-Saint-Michel and Chartres*, included several negative references to such characters as "Jew [art] dealers" and "Jew theatremanagers" (1905: 179, 279).

Adams was much blunter in his personal letters. Selected comments include the following:

1893: "With a communism I could exist tolerable well, for the commune is rather favorable to social consideration apart from wealth; but in a society of Jews and brokers, a world made up of maniacs wild for gold, I have no place. In the coming [battles], you will know where to find me. Probably I shall be helping the London mob to pull up Harcourt and Rothschild on a lamp-post in Piccadilly".[13]

1894: "I am myself more than ever at odds with my time. I detest it, and everything that belongs to it, and live only in the wish to see the end of it, with all its infernal Jewry. I want to put every money lender to death, and to sink Lombard Street and Wall Street under the ocean".[14]

1896: "America is horribly in debt to Europe. … A large portion of this—no one can even guess how large—is floating capital, all practically Jew money, and lent practically on call. … In this situation an investment is sheer gambling. We are in the hands of the Jews. They can do what they please with our values".[15]

---

[13] Letter to Charles Gaskell, dated 15 September 1893; in Adams (1969: 33). William Vernon Harcourt was the non-Jewish Chancellor of the Exchequer. The "Rothschild" to which he refers is likely Nathan Mayer Rothschild, prominent Jewish banker and politician.

[14] In Samuels (1964: 129).

[15] Letter to Charles Gaskell, dated 31 July 1896; in Adams (1969: 110-111).

1896: "The Jew has got into the soul. I see him—or her—now everywhere, and wherever he—or she—goes, there must remain a taint in the blood forever".[16]

1896: "I tell you Rome was a blessed garden of paradise beside the rotten, unsexed, swindling, lying Jews, represented by Pierpont Morgan and the gang who have been manipulating the country for the last four years".[17]

1898: "[The Dreyfus Affair] has resulted in enormously stimulating the anti-Semite feeling in France, which has reached the point where violence has become only a matter of time. ... For no one doubts now that the whole campaign has been one of money and intrigue; and the French are very furious. Of course, all the English and the Americans are with the Jews, which makes it worse..."[18]

1899: "[In Paris,] there are a thousand bric-a-brac dealers, and all have hopeless rubbish, except three or four Jews who force up prices by cornering fashions. Anything these Jews touch is in some strange way vulgarized. One does not want it anymore. It has become a trade..."[19]

1899: "Joe Chamberlain has, apparently, got to make a war such as must make his hair stand on end. ... But our interests require that the Boers should be brought into our system, and so we must kill them till they come; because all England and all America and all the Transvaal are a Jew interest—that is, a great capitalist machine—and we must run it, no matter whom it hurts".[20]

---

[16] In Samuels (1964: 168).

[17] In Samuels (1964: 169). Pierpont ("J. P.") Morgan was the leading, and non-Jewish, banker of the day. But he evidently had a team of Jewish bankers working for him.

[18] Letter to Elizabeth Cameron, dated 13 January 1898; in Adams (1969: 145).

[19] Letter to Charles Gaskell, dated June 1899; in Adams (1969: 233).

[20] Letter to Elizabeth Cameron, dated 18 September 1899; in Adams (1969: 241). Joseph Chamberlain was British Secretary of State. The conflict to which

> 1914: "The atmosphere [in Washington DC] really has become a
> Jew atmosphere. It is curious and evidently good for some people,
> but it isolates me. ... We keep Jews far away, and the anti-Jew
> feeling is quite rabid. ... [Y]et we somehow seem to be more Jew-
> ish every day".[21]

Adams died in 1918, living long enough to witness the end of World
War I. But he evidently made few further comments on the Jews.

Adams' friend and younger contemporary, Henry James, also
commented negatively on the Jews, mostly in his fictional works. For
example, a short story of 1896, "Glasses," includes this passage: "There
were thousands of little chairs and almost as many little Jews; and there
was music in an open rotunda, over which the little Jews wagged their
big noses" (1996: 525). Additionally, James' major nonfiction book *The
American Scene* (1907) included this biting assessment of the "Yiddish
quarter" of New York City:

> There is no swarming like that of Israel when once Israel
> has got a start, and the scene here bristled, at every step,
> with the signs and sounds, immitigable, unmistakable, of a
> Jewry that had burst all bounds. ... It was as if we had been
> thus...at the bottom of some vast sallow aquarium in which
> innumerable fish, of over-developed proboscis, were to
> bump together, for ever, amid heaped spoils of the sea.
> (1968: 131)

He continues in his biological metaphors when speaking of the Jewish
Diaspora:

> Is it simply...that the unsurpassed strength of the race per-
> mits of the chopping into myriads of fine fragments without
> loss of race-quality? There are small, strange animals,
> known to natural history, snakes or worms, I believe, who,
> when cut into pieces, wriggle away contentedly and live in

Adams refers would become known as the Second Boer War (1899-1902); the
early campaigns were disastrous for Britain, but eventually they triumphed.
[21] Letter to Charles Gaskell, dated 19 February 1914; in Adams (1969: 620).

the snippet as completely as in the whole. So the denizens of the New York City Ghetto...had each…his or her own share of the whole hard glitter of Israel.

Academic Confirmation

For the most part, these many negative observations find confirmation in the work of social scientists of the time. A notable example is Edward A. Ross, who was a sociology professor at several American universities around the turn of the century. He published an important book in 1914, titled *The Old World in the New*, which examined social characteristics of several immigrant ethnicities. One chapter is dedicated to "the East European Hebrews." Though only one of several ethnic groups, Ross writes of "the endeavor of the Jews to control immigration policy of the United States" (1914: 144). "The systematic campaign in newspapers and magazines," he adds, "to break down all arguments for restriction…is waged by and for one race." Jews, he observes, will force open national borders to all varieties of undesirable types, simply to allow in more Jews: "In order to admit their brethren…the brightest of the Semites are keeping our doors open to the dullest of the Aryans!"[22] Again, the parallels to the present day are striking.

Not all Jews are morally objectionable, writes Ross, but "certain bad qualities crop out all too often among these eastern Europeans" (149). New York social workers "testify that no other immigrants are so noisy, pushing, and disdainful of the rights of others as the Hebrews." Not only that, but they are itinerant law-breakers; "authorities complain that the East European Hebrews feel no reverence for the law as such, and are willing to break any ordinance they find in their way"—a sentiment surely applicable to the leading Jewish figures today. Jewish merchants are derided as "slippery," often claiming bankruptcy simply to escape debt. Generally speaking, the immorality of Jewish businessmen is common knowledge. In a revealing passage, Ross writes:

---

[22] Ross' use of the word 'Aryan' is notable, given that this was some two decades prior to the rise of National Socialism. It demonstrates that the term had currency in intellectual circles.

> It is charged that, for personal gain, the Jewish dealer willfully disregards the customs of the trade and thereby throws trade ethics into confusion. Physicians and lawyers complain that their Jewish colleagues tend to break down the ethics of their professions. It is certain that Jews have commercialized the social evil, commercialized the theater, and done much to commercialize the newspaper. (153)

"Most alarming," continues Ross, "is the great increase in criminality among Jewish young men, and the growth of prostitution among Jewish girls" (155). Jews themselves even admit these problems, and that they are self-caused. Ross quotes a Hebrew politician: "It [prevalent Jewish immorality] was a product of cold, calculating, mercenary methods, devised and handled by men of Jewish birth." Jewish criminality is made all the worse by the fact that they are exceptionally clever:

> With his clear brain sharpened in the American school, the egoistic, conscienceless young Jew constitutes a menace. As a Jewish labor leader said to me, "the non-morality of the young Jewish businessmen is fearful." (157)

Of special interest is the Jewish tendency to bend the truth. "For lying, the immigrant has a very bad reputation. In the North End of Boston, 'the readiness of the Jews to commit perjury has passed into proverb'." Ross notes that immigration officials are frequently subject to false accusations in the Jewish press, and that US senators are "overwhelmed with a torrent of crooked statistics and misrepresentations" (150).

Ross concludes that Jewish immigrants arrive here as "moral cripples," "haters of government," and "corrupters of police." "Many of them," furthermore, "have developed a monstrous and repulsive love of [financial] gain." Immorality thus combines with greed, and the result is predictable:

> When now, they use their Old-World shove and wile and lie in a society like ours, as unprotected as a snail out of its shell, they rapidly push up into a position of prosperous parasitism, leaving scorn and curses in their wake. (154)

There we have it: Clever, shifty, hostile, conniving Jews exploit a relatively open and innocent populace; they acquire wealth and power; and thereby they corrupt and degrade all aspects of society. They are, indeed, "prosperous parasites" in our midst. One could scarcely ask for a more apt summary of the situation. This is all the more forceful, given that it comes from not an alleged anti-Semite but a prominent university professor. Where is such academic courage today, when it is needed the most?

CHAPTER 8

AMERICAN VIEWS IN WARTIME

Theodore Dreiser and Henry Louis (H. L.) Mencken were erstwhile friends, mutual critics, and occasional enemies, but the two American writers shared a critical view of the Jews. Rather like Shaw's case, Dreiser's notable anti-Semitic reputation rests almost completely on a single letter published in *American Spectator* magazine in October 1933. As a co-editor, Dreiser had initiated a symposium on the Jewish Question, inviting comment from readers. A pro-Semitic contribution by a non-Jew, Hutchins Hapgood, drew a sharp reply from Dreiser:

> Liberality has always had a dubious standing in my mental court. … Liberalism, in the case of the Jew, means internationalism. He is to wander where he pleases and retain, as he does, his religion and race characteristics without change. The Jews…are by preference lawyers, bankers, merchants, money-lenders and brokers, and middlemen. If you listen to Jews discuss Jews, you will find that they are money-minded, very pagan, very sharp in practice, and, usually, in so far as the rest is concerned, they have the single objective of plenty of money, by means of which they build a fairly material surrounding.
>
> The profession of the law is today seriously considering …limiting the number of Jewish lawyers…for a very definite reason. The Jews lack…the fine integrity which at least is endorsed and, to a degree, followed by the lawyers of other nationalities. At least, that is the charge. Left to sheer liberalism as you interpret it, they could possess America by sheer numbers, their cohesion, and their race tastes, and …really overrun the land.
>
> The Jew insists that when he invades Italy or France or America or what you will, he becomes a native of that country—a full-blooded native of that country. You know yourself, if you know anything, that that is not true. He has

been in Germany now for all of a thousand years, if not
longer, and he is still a Jew. He has been in America all of
two hundred years, and he has not faded into a pure American by any means, and he will not.

[Thus,] liberalism might be willing to step aside at least
to the extent of suggesting to or even advising the Jew to
undertake a land of his own. I say this because I am for nationalism as opposed to internationalism...[1]

Dreiser speaks the harsh truth, and furthermore promotes the Zionist
cause as a means for relieving Jewish cultural pressure on European and
American societies. In reply, Hapgood accuses him of not only being
anti-Semitic, but Jew-hating, Jew-baiting, and as serving as no better
than "a representative of Hitler." Dreiser wrote a second reply in December of that year, denying that he wanted Jews removed from America.
Yet still, he endorsed the call for "an international conference with all
Jewry" to solve once and for all the Jewish Question. The Jews, he insists,

are mistaken in attempting to establish themselves as Jews
...in the bosom, not of any one country or people, but rather in the lands of almost every country the world over...
It is not reasonable. It is not the way—especially since, being as gifted as they are, they so rapidly rise to power and
affluence wherever they go.[2]

He concludes by again explicitly endorsing the Zionist cause as a best
solution.

Mencken's situation was comparable to Dreiser's: rare but blunt
talk about the Jews, combined with an unapologetic attitude. Mencken's
most notorious comments came in his 1930 nonfiction book *Treatise on
the Gods*. The work is an insightful and well-argued rationalist critique of
all major religions; Christianity is the main target, but the Jewish religion
comes in for its share of abuse: "The Old Testament, as everyone who has
looked into it is aware, drips with blood; ... Yahweh's revelations to

---

[1] Dreiser (1933a). Reprinted in Dreiser (1959: 651). Also reprinted in H.
Hapgood, "Is Dreiser anti-Semitic?," *Nation* (17 April, 1935), 436.
[2] Dreiser (1933b). Reprinted in Hapgood, ibid., 437-438.

Moses commanded an almost continuous butchery" (1930: 158). The Jews, he said, were "a naturally rebellious and contentious people" (257). Hence, "Judaism, as a practical cult, is made ridiculous by an archaic and ridiculous ritualism and by a code of ethics that goes back to savagery" (343).

But it was the following passage that caused the most ruckus. The Bible, said Mencken, was a beautiful and poetic (and fictional) book, and thus it is rather amazing that it was composed by the Jewish race: "For there is little in their character, as the modern world knows them, to suggest a talent for noble thinking." He then added this striking remark:

> One might go still further. The Jews could be put down very plausibly as the most unpleasant race ever heard of. As commonly encountered, they lack many of the qualities that mark civilized man: courage, dignity, incorruptibility, ease, confidence. They have vanity without pride, voluptuousness without taste, and learning without wisdom. Their fortitude, such as it is, is wasted on puerile objects, and their charity is mainly only a form of display. (345-346)

Similar—though even harsher—thoughts recur in an undated personal note:

> The sharp, unyielding separateness of the Jews, based on their assertive racial egoism, marks them off as strangers everywhere… The chief whooping for what is called racial tolerance comes from the Jews, who are the most intolerable people on earth. In the United States, as in all countries in which they inhabit, they interpret tolerance to mean only an active support of their own special interests… [T]he average Jew leaves one no alternative. He is Jewish before he is a man, and presses the fact home with relentless lack of tact.[3]

…comments that strike one as being every bit as valid today as when they were written.

---

[3] In Teachout (2002: 189-190).

Mencken's last work, *Minority Report*, consists of a series of short observations and aphorisms. Two of these reflect on Judaism. The first offers this assessment: "I am one of the few Goyim who have ever actually tackled the Talmud. ... It seems to me, save for a few bright spots, to be quite indistinguishable from rubbish" (1956: 148). Then near the end of the book, we find this broader remark:

> The Jewish theory that Goyim envy the superior ability of Jews is not borne out by the facts. Most Goyim, in fact, deny that the Jew is superior, and point in evidence to his failure to take the first prizes: he has to be content with the seconds. No Jewish composer has ever come within miles of Bach, Beethoven and Brahms, no Jew has ever challenged the top-flight painters of the world, and no Jewish scientist has ever equaled Newton, Darwin, Pasteur, or Mendel. In the latter bracket such apparent exceptions as Ehrlich, Freud and Einstein are only apparent. Ehrlich, in fact, contributed less to biochemical fact than to biochemical theory, and most of his theory was dubious. Freud was nine-tenths quack, and there is sound reason for believing that even Einstein will not hold up... The Goy does not, in fact, believe that the Jew is better than the non-Jew; the most he will admit is that the Jew is smarter at achieving worldly success. But this he ascribes to sharp practices, and not to superior abilities. (273-274)

One final figure of note from the interwar period was American (turned British) poet and essayist T. S. Eliot. His small book *After Strange Gods* addresses the importance of cultural unity and cohesiveness. "Stability is obviously necessary," he writes, and "the population should be homogenous." But he adds:

> What is still more important is unity of religious background; and reasons of race and religion combine to make any large number of free-thinking Jews undesirable. (1934: 20)

It's an odd passage. There is no elaboration. The reference to the Jews is seemingly arbitrary, and it is the sole mention in the entire book. But it does mark another instance in a sporadic history for Eliot of making such passing references. His 1919 poem "Burbank with a Baedeker," a short, impressionistic piece, includes these lines: "The rats are underneath the piles. / The jew is underneath the lot. / Money in furs." One year later, in his poem "Gerontion," he writes: "My house is a decayed house / and the jew squats on the window sill…" Another short poem of the same year, "Sweeney among the Nightingales," includes this phrase: "Rachel née Rabinovich / Tears at the grapes with murderous paws"; two stanzas later Eliot mentions a man with "a golden grin" (Jews = gold). Such obscure and vaguely critical allusions would pass unnoticed for any ethnicity other than Jews. But a handful of such lines are enough to permanently tar him with the anti-Semite label.[4]

Ford on the Jews

The Second World War obviously brought many aspects of Jewish influence to the fore, but even earlier, in the interwar period, notable figures were making critical comments. Henry Ford was an anti-war activist most of his life, beginning with WWI. In December of 1915, just as that war had commenced, he chartered a 'peace ship' on a journey to Norway to convene a peace conference. He explains:

> On that ship were two very prominent Jews. We had not been to sea 200 miles before these two Jews began telling me about the power of the Jewish race, how they controlled the world through their control of gold, and that the Jew, and no one but the Jew, could stop the war.
>
> I was reluctant to believe this, and said so…so they went into detail to tell me the means by which the Jew con-

---

[4] Incredibly, one Anthony Julius was able to scrape together literally a half-dozen such passages and turn them into an entire book: *T. S. Eliot, Anti-Semitism, and Literary Form* (1995/2003). This book is a kind of masterpiece of reading between lines and intuiting hidden intentions. The reader is invited to read Eliot's allegedly anti-Semitic poems—"Gerontion," "A Cooking Egg," "Sweeney among the Nightingales," "The Waste Land"—and judge for himself.

trolled the war, how they had the money, how they had cornered all the basic materials needed to fight the war, and all that, and they talked so long and so well that they convinced me. They said, and they believed, that the Jews started the war; that they would continue it as long as they wished, and that until the Jew stopped the war it could not be stopped. We were in mid-ocean and I was so disgusted that I would have liked to have turned the ship back.[5]

Thus, "it was the Jews themselves that convinced me of the direct relation between the international Jew and war..." The peace mission was a failure, but even during his short time in Europe, Ford "could see that a lot of the things the Jews had told me were so."

A few years later, in 1919, he was making his first public statements on the topic. "International financiers are behind all war... [T]hey are what is called the international Jew: German Jews, French Jews, English Jews, American Jews...the Jew is a threat".[6]

Around that same time, Ford evidently decided to get his message out to the American people, but found that "no newspaper in the United States...dared print the truth." So he bought his own paper—the *Dearborn Independent*—and began a two-year series of weekly articles exposing their misdeeds in government, finance, business, religion, culture, sports, and many other aspects of American society. Ford relied on a two-man team, William Cameron and Ernest Liebold, to research and write the weekly pieces, all of which presumably ran with Ford's endorsement. The first issue, dated 22 May 1920, was headlined "The International Jew: The World's Problem." Thereafter followed a string of insightful and well-written critiques, 87 pieces in all, each about 4,000 words in length, and each tackling in detail some aspect of the Jewish Question.

It is an astonishing series of articles, particularly for a popular news weekly. Academic works are quoted, experts cited, names are named. The various essays have been combined into book form, most recently in

---

[5] *New York Times*, 5 Dec 1921, p. 33.
[6] In Wallace (2003: 7).

2024.[7] A few quotations from selected articles give a good feel for the reasoned but critical tone:

- "It is not merely that there are a few Jews among international financial controllers; it is that these world controllers are exclusively Jews." (ch. 1)

- "Germany is today, with perhaps the possible exception of the United States, the most Jew-controlled country in the world—controlled within and from without." (ch. 14)

- "Not only the 'legitimate' stage, so-called, but the motion picture industry—the fifth greatest of all the great industries—is also Jew-controlled, not in spots only, not 50 percent merely, *but entirely.*" (ch. 33)

- "What principally makes it [Jewish dominance] a menace? This —that the stage today represents the principal cultural element of 50 percent of the public. What the average young person absorbs as to good form, proper deportment, refinement as contrasted with coarseness, correctness of speech or choice of words, customs and feelings of other nations, even fashions of clothes, as well as ideas of religion and law, are derived from what he sees and hears at the theater. The masses' sole idea of the homes and the life of the rich is derived from the stage and the movies. More wrong notions are given, more prejudices created by the Jewish-controlled theater in one week, than can be charged against a serious study of the Jewish Question in a century. People sometimes wonder where the ideas of the younger generation come from. This is the answer." (ch. 34)

- "The Jews do not believe in free speech. They do not believe in a free press." (ch. 37)

---

[7] *The International Jew: The Definitive Edition* (two volumes), by Henry Ford (T. Dalton, ed.; Clemens & Blair; 2024).

- "It is rather surprising, is it not, that whichever way you turn to trace the harmful streams of influence that flow through society, you come upon a group of Jews? In baseball corruption—a group of Jews. In exploitative finance—a group of Jews. In theatrical degeneracy—a group of Jews. In liquor propaganda—a group of Jews. In control of national war policies—a group of Jews. Absolutely dominating the wireless communications of the world—a group of Jews. In the menace of the movies—a group of Jews. In control of the press through business and financial pressure—a group of Jews. War profiteers, 80 percent of them—Jews. Organizers of active opposition of Christian laws and customs—Jews. And now, in this miasma of so-called popular music, which combines weak-mindedness with every suggestion of lewdness—again Jews. ... There is something Satanic about it, something calculated with demonic shrewdness." (ch. 64)

- "If you could put a tag marked 'Jewish' on every part of your life that is Jew-controlled, you would be astonished at the showing." (ch. 65)

- "If you want to know which way Jewry is going and where is the hiding of its power, watch the Zionists." (ch. 66)

- "The fact is that a sport is clean and helpful until it begins to attract Jewish investors and exploiters, and then it goes bad. The two facts have occurred in pairs too frequently and under too many dissimilar circumstances to have their relationship doubted." (ch. 68)

- "The maintenance of the idea of drink in the minds of the people is due to Jewish propaganda. There is not a dialogue on the stage today that does not drip with whisky patter. As all the plays making much noise this year are not only Jew-written, Jew-produced, and Jew-controlled, but also Jew-played (the stage swarms with Jewish faces this year), the drip of whisky patter is constant. If theatergoers were at all observant, they would see that most of their money goes to support pro-Jewish propaganda in one form or another, which, is of course, a tribute to Jewish business genius—what other people could embark on a pro-racial propaganda and make the opposite race pay for it?" (ch. 85)

- "It was exactly like these days when we are told that 'American businessmen' abroad are doing terrible things; yet even while the press declares them to be 'American' we cannot understand how Americans could do such things—and we never get the key to the matter, nor see the solution, until we stumble on to the fact that these so-called 'Americans' are not Americans at all, but alien Jews. Over in Canada, the name 'American' is becoming a stigma because it is borne by men who are not Americans. What Canadians point out in the United States as definitely 'American' is mostly Jewish, but how are the Canadians to know? The national name suffers. The whole cause of evil is camouflaged and a nation pays the price of a racial group's misdeeds. There should be some method of protecting this forging of national names." (ch. 72)

- "Take anti-Semitism. That is a label which the Jews have industriously pasted up everywhere. If ever it was an effective label, its uses are over now. It doesn't mean anything." (ch. 78)

- "[A] Jew scents fear a long way; the man who fears, even though he fear to be unfair, is already marked by the Jew who may happen to be stationed to watch him." (ch. 79)

- "There was very little left at the end…except to assume that the Jews were a sacrosanct race, with special privileges, a race whom no non-Jews should presume even to mention in anything but awe-filled tones." (ch. 79)

… even as they commit the most heinous of crimes, whether against Whites, or downtrodden Palestinians, or other non-Jews around the world. All in all, a remarkable accomplishment by one of the richest men in the world in the 1920s.

Ford concisely summarized his thoughts in a 1922 biography, *My Life and Work*, composed just as the International Jew series came to a close:

> The work which we describe as Studies in the Jewish Question, and which is variously described by antagonists as "the Jewish campaign," "the attack on the Jews," "the anti-Semitic pogrom," and so forth, needs no explanation to those who have followed it. Its motives and purposes must be judged by the work itself. It is offered as a contribution to a question which deeply affects the country, a question which is racial at its source and which concerns influences and ideals rather than persons. Our statements must be judged by candid readers who are intelligent enough to lay our words alongside life as they are able to observe it. If our word and their observation agree, the case is made. It is perfectly silly to begin to damn us before it has been shown that our statements are baseless or reckless. The first item to be considered is the truth of what we have set forth. And that is precisely the item which our critics choose to evade.

This is an important point, often overlooked even today. Present-day critics of Jews are roundly condemned and slandered, and yet virtually never does the Jewish apologist address the factual basis of the complaint. It is too inconvenient, and too embarrassing, for Jews or Jewish defenders to accept and respond to the facts of the matter at hand. Ford continues:

> Readers of our articles will see at once that we are not actuated by any kind of prejudice, except it may be a prejudice in favor of the principles which have made our civilization. There had been observed in this country certain streams of influence which were causing a marked deterioration in our literature, amusements, and social conduct; business was departing from its old-time substantial soundness; a general letting down of standards was felt everywhere. It was not the robust coarseness of the white man, the rude indelicacy, say, of Shakespeare's characters, but a nasty Orientalism

which has insidiously affected every channel of expression—and to such an extent that it was time to challenge it.
The fact that these influences are all traceable to one racial
source is a fact to be reckoned with, not by us only, but by
the intelligent people of the race in question...

Our work does not pretend to say the last word on the
Jew in America. It says only the word which describes his
obvious present impress on the country. When that impress
is changed, the report of it can be changed. For the present,
then, the question is wholly in the Jews' hands. If they are
as wise as they claim to be, they will labor to make Jews
American, instead of laboring to make America Jewish.
(1998: 250-251)

Charles Lindbergh: American Hero

As a close friend of Henry Ford and a fellow peace advocate, Charles
Lindbergh also identified the Jews as a cause of war. Following his historic transatlantic flight in 1927 at age 25 and his move to Europe in
1935, Lindbergh promoted the peaceful development of aviation tech-
nologies. From 1936 to 1938 he made several visits to Germany, and it
was during this time that he first encountered impoverished Jews heading
to the US. Shortly after *Kristallnacht* he was at a train station in Paris,
and recorded the following thoughts in his diary:

> The station platform is filled with Jews leaving for Ameri-
> ca. They were a poor looking lot on the whole... I have
> never been anti-Jewish and have great respect and admira-
> tion for Jews I know. Some of them are among my best
> friends. But this group on the station platform gave me a
> strange feeling of pity and disgust. These people are bound
> to cause trouble if many of them go to America.[8]

Less than a year later, war in Europe was imminent—though the US had
no obvious stake in it, and even England was arguably best served by

---

[8] Entry dated 19 Nov 1938. In Wallace (2003: 382).

disengagement. On 30 June 1939, Lindbergh had a short meeting with vice president John Garner to discuss developments. Again from his diary:

> We are both anxious to avoid having this country pushed into a European war by British and Jewish propaganda, of which there is already too much. ... [T]here is far too much at stake for us to rush into a European war without the most careful and cool consideration. (1970: 218)

Two months later, over a dinner meeting with prominent journalist Fulton Lewis, Lindbergh discussed America's reaction if war were to break out:

> We are disturbed about the effect of the Jewish influence in our press, radio, and motion pictures. It may become very serious. ... I fear that trouble lies ahead in this regard. Whenever the Jewish percentage of the population becomes too high, a reaction seems to invariably occur. It is too bad because a few Jews of the right type are, I believe, an asset to any country, adding to rather than detracting from its strength. If an anti-Semitic movement starts in the United States, it may go far. It will certainly affect the good Jews along with the others. When such a movement starts, moderation ends.[9]

One week later, war began between Germany and Poland. It became a European-wide conflict two days after that, when England and France declared war on Germany—and not vice versa. Through all of 1940, Germany rolled up gains across the continent, taking Paris in mid-June. Pressure grew for American involvement, and Lindbergh continued to work for an isolationist, anti-war stance. In the middle of 1941, he again addressed the topic of the incessant 'British-Jewish propaganda':

> The pressure for war is high and mounting. The people are opposed to it, but the [Roosevelt] Administration seems to have "the bit in its teeth" and hell-bent on its way to war.

---

[9] In Wallace (2003: 199).

> Most of the Jewish interests in the country are behind war, and they control a huge part of our press and radio and most of our motion pictures. There are also the "intellectuals," and the "Anglophiles," and the British agents who are allowed free rein, the international financial interests, and many others. (1970: 481)

A few months later, a momentous event: Lindbergh's speech in Des Moines, Iowa, on 11 September 1941.[10] There he discussed the "over-increasing effort" to push the US into war, "carried on by foreign interests, and by a small minority of our own people".[11] "Who is responsible?" he asked, proceeding to identify the top three culprits: *the British, the Jews,* and *the Roosevelt administration.* It is worth noting—though Lindbergh did not—that in fact Jews were behind the actions of both Churchill and Roosevelt; in a sense, then, one could point to them as the *primary* source of US engagement.

Taking the three in turn, he comes to the Jews:

> It is not difficult to understand why Jewish people desire the overthrow of Nazi Germany. The persecution they suffered in Germany would be sufficient to make bitter enemies of any race.
>
> No person with a sense of the dignity of mankind can condone the persecution of the Jewish race in Germany. But no person of honesty and vision can look on their pro-war policy here today without seeing the dangers involved in such a policy both for us and for them. Instead of agitating for war, the Jewish groups in this country should be opposing it in every possible way, for they will be among the first to feel its consequences.
>
> Tolerance is a virtue that depends upon peace and strength. History shows that it cannot survive war and devastations. A few far-sighted Jewish people realize this and stand opposed to intervention. But the majority still do not.

---

[10] Oddly, 60 years to the day before that other "9/11".
[11] Full text online at: www.charleslindbergh.com.

Their greatest danger to this country lies in their large own-
ership and influence in our motion pictures, our press, our
radio, and our government.

I am not attacking either the Jewish or the British people. Both races, I admire. But I am saying that the leaders
of both the British and the Jewish races, for reasons which
are as understandable from their viewpoint as they are in-
advisable from ours, for reasons which are not American,
wish to involve us in the war.

We cannot blame them for looking out for what they
believe to be their own interests, but we also must look out
for ours. We cannot allow the natural passions and prejudices of other peoples to lead our country to destruction.

Lindbergh then adds that none of the three alone are capable of forcing
the US into war, only the combined action of all. He describes a three-
step process in the push forward, the first two of which—promotion of
American "defense interests" and incremental involvement—were already
complete. Only the third step awaited: the creation of "a series of incidents
which would force us into actual conflict"—a striking statement, given
that the Pearl Harbor attack would happen just three months later.

In his diary of that day, Lindbergh (1970: 538) remarked, "When I
mentioned the three major groups agitating for war—the British, the
Jewish, and the Roosevelt administration—the entire audience seemed to
stand and cheer." But amongst the American press, the response was
predictable. "The *New York Times* carries bitter attacks on my address
from Jewish and other organizations," he wrote on 13 September.[12] And
two days later: "I felt I had worded my Des Moines address carefully and
moderately. It seems that almost anything can be discussed today in

---

[12] Two articles that day attacked him. Prominent socialist Norman Thomas was
sympathetic with his anti-war position, but said, "No race or people can be
made the scapegoat…" Another article quoted critiques by a government
spokesman (equating Lindbergh's words with the Nazis'), two New York
committees, a Supreme Court justice, and the president of the Women's Zionist Organization. A Protestant journalist is quoted as saying, "Anti-Semitism is
anti-Christianity," and, "This Lindbergh speech is the beginning of the last
phase of a definite plan to destroy democratic government in this country."

America except the Jewish problem. The very mention of the word 'Jew' is cause for a storm." Indeed.

September 18 was his last diary entry on the subject:

> [America First executive] John Flynn came at 11:00, and we talked the situation over for an hour. Flynn says he does not question the truth of what I said at Des Moines, but feels it was inadvisable to mention the Jewish problem. It is difficult for me to understand Flynn's attitude. He feels as strongly as I do that the Jews are among the major influences pushing this country toward war. He has said so frequently, and he says so now. He is perfectly willing to talk about it among a small group of people in private. But apparently he would rather see us get into the war than mention in public what the Jews are doing, no matter how tolerantly and moderately it is done.
>
> On the other hand, I feel: (1) that the people of this country should know what Jewish influence is doing; and (2) that the Jews should be warned of the result they will bring onto their shoulders if they continue their present course.[13]

This was apparently his final reference to the Jews, either in public or private. By December of 1941, the US was in the war and there was no turning back.

Postwar Reflections

Soon after the end of WW2, American president Harry Truman (1997: 41) wrote the following observation in his diary: "The Jews claim God Almighty picked them out for special privilege. Well, I'm sure He had better judgment." Two years later, in a diary entry of 21 July 1947, Truman was more explicit:

> The Jews have no sense of proportion nor do they have any judgment on world affairs. … The Jews, I find, are very,

---

[13] Combined from passages in Lindbergh (1970: 541) and Wallace (2003: 382).

very selfish. They care not how many Estonians, Latvians, Finns, Poles, Yugoslavs or Greeks get murdered or mistreated as DP [displaced persons] as long as the Jews get special treatment. Yet when they have power—physical, financial or political—neither Hitler nor Stalin has anything on them for cruelty or mistreatment to the underdog.[14]

The end of the war brought numerous problems, not the least of which was how to handle the masses of displaced persons (DPs), most of whom were Jews. American generals, including Eisenhower and George S. Patton, had to manage the awkward situation. Patton did not relish this task, at least when it came to the Jews, whom he considered to be in far worse shape than the other DPs. This was not due to their harsh treatment by the Germans, which, for those who survived, was not measurably worse than other persecuted ethnicities; rather, it was a result of the feeble constitution of the Jewish people themselves. Patton's diary of 15 September 1945 records the following:

> Harrison and his associates indicate that they feel German civilians should be removed from houses for the purposes of housing Displaced Persons. ... Harrison and his ilk believe that the Displaced Person is a human being, which he is not, and this applies particularly to the Jews who are lower than animals. I remember once at Troina in Sicily, General Gay said that it wasn't a question of the people living with the dirty animals but of the animals living with the dirty people. At that time, he had never seen a Displaced Jew.
>
> Furthermore, I do not see why Jews should be treated any better or any worse than Catholics, Protestants, Mohammedans, or Mormons. However, it seems apparent that we will have to do this... (1974: 751-752)

Things got worse for Patton a couple days later:

---

[14] See: www.jewishvirtuallibrary.org/truman-diary-entry-disparages-jews.

We drove for about 45 minutes to a Jewish camp... The buildings were in a good state of repair when the Jews arrived but were in a bad state of repair when we arrived, because these Jewish DPs, or at least a majority of them, have no sense of human relationships. They decline, where practicable, to use latrines, preferring to relieve themselves on the floor...

This happened to be the feast of Yom Kippur, so they were all collected in a large wooden building which they called a synagogue. It behooved General Eisenhower to make a speech to them. We entered the synagogue which was packed with the greatest stinking bunch of humanity I have ever seen. When we got about half way up, the head rabbi, who was dressed in a fur hat similar to that worn by Henry VIII of England and in a surplice heavily embroidered and very filthy, came down and met the General. Also a copy of the Talmud, I think it is called, written on a sheet and rolled around a stick, was carried by one of the attending physicians.

First, a Jewish civilian made a very long speech which nobody seemed inclined to translate. Then General Eisenhower mounted the platform and I went up behind him, and he made a short and excellent speech, which was translated paragraph by paragraph.

However, the smell was so terrible that I almost fainted and actually about three hours later lost my lunch as the result of remembering it. (753-754)

The infamous *foetor Judaicus* returns with a vengeance! On 21 September, fellow general Louis Craig inspected another Jewish camp; according to Patton, "He said the conditions and filth were unspeakable. … My personal opinion is that no people could have sunk to the level of degradation these have reached in the short space of four years" (759).

Within 10 days, the army had begun the process of moving the Jews to new quarters: "Again we ran into the sub-human characteristics of these people in that they do not understand toilets, and refuse to use them except as repositories for tin cans, garbage, and refuse…" (788). Patton coordinated efforts with the UN Relief and Rehabilitation Administration (UNRRA), who took care not only of Jews but all DPs:

> The UNRRA woman informed me without solicitation that the Estonians detailed to cut wood for the camp cut four times as much wood per day as did the Jews. She believes, and I think with some show of veracity, that the Jews are in a psychopathic condition which may be materially improved, although personally I doubt it. I have never looked at a group of people who seem to be more lacking in intelligence and spirit. Practically all of them had the flat brownish gray eye common among the Hawaiians which, to my mind, indicates very low intelligence.
>
> Owing to the cooler weather, the smell of the inhabitants was below average but still extremely nauseating to western nostrils. It is an unfortunate fact that the people at home who are so vociferous in their demands for the betterment of the Displaced Jews have no conception of the low mental, moral, and physical standards of the objects of their solicitude…

The "vociferousness" of the Americans was due, in large part, to a Jewish presence in the media: "There is a very apparent Semitic influence in the press" (766). Patton was evidently depressed by the whole affair: "The more I see of people, I regret that I survived the war."

In fact, Patton would not survive much longer. He was involved in a minor auto accident on 9 December 1945, was taken to a military hospital, was recovering, but then mysteriously died on December 21 at the age of 60. Conspiracy theorists believe he was murdered on account of his impolitic views.[15]

In his anti-Jewish sentiments, Patton was not alone among the military leadership. Another WW2 general, George Moseley, was yet more strident. Even before the war, in early 1939, Moseley openly said that "the war now proposed is for the purpose of establishing Jewish hegem-

---

[15] See the book *Target: Patton*, by R. Wilcox (2008) for more details—but precious little on any potential Jewish role.

ony throughout the world".[16] And on 1 June 1939 he testified before the House Un-American Activities Committee, condemning "world Jewry" and arguing that American Jews should be disenfranchised because of their primary allegiance to a global Jewish state.[17] For some reason, these observations by major American generals have been lost to history.

---

[16] In Bendersky (2000: 255).
[17] See the recap in the *New York Times*, 2 June (p. 8).

CHAPTER 9

TO THE PRESENT DAY

They're a filthy, lying, bastard people...
Study the history.
—Chess master Bobby Fischer (1999)

After World War Two, and upon the emergence of American global he-gemony, Jewish influence became truly dominant for the first time in history. The Holocaust story was developed and promoted, providing moral, political, and financial support for Jewish (now Israeli) actions in all spheres.[1] American foreign aid to Israel grew to more than $6 billion annually, without comment and without challenge. American media, enter-tainment, academia, and finance all became directly or indirectly dominated by Jewish interests. US politics became deeply corrupted by Jewish money and the power of lobbying groups such as AIPAC.[2]

In 1974, another American general and chairman of the Joint Chiefs of Staff, George Brown, made some blunt statements along these lines. During a speech of October 10, he said that the power of the Jewish lob-by "was so strong you wouldn't believe it." He continued:

> [The Israelis say] "Don't worry about Congress. We'll take care of Congress." Now, this is somebody from another country, but they can do it. They own, you know, the banks in this country, the newspapers, you just look at where the Jewish money is in this country.[3]

---

[1] For a critical study, see Dalton, *Debating the Holocaust* (4th ed., 2020) or, in more concise form, *The Holocaust: 100 Questions and Answers* (2025) or *The Holocaust: An Introduction* (2016).

[2] For an overview of the central facts, see either Dalton (2020: 263-282) or the Introduction in Hitler (2024).

[3] In Bendersky (2000: 428). Also quoted in *The Washington Post*, 13 Nov 1974 (p. A1).

If Americans really were serious, Brown said, they would set out to "break that lobby." In that same year, President Richard Nixon voiced similar concerns:

> There may be some truth in that if the Arabs have some complaints about my policy towards Israel, they have to realize that the Jews in the US control the entire information and propaganda machine, the large newspapers, the motion pictures, radio and television, and the big companies. And there is a force that we have to take into consideration.[4]

But Nixon had long had concerns about Jewish influence in America. In a taped recording in the White House in 1971, he expressed his dissatisfaction at the fact that Jews were leading the push for legalization of marijuana: "Every one of the bastards that are out for legalizing marijuana is Jewish. What the Christ is the matter with the Jews, Bob? What is the matter with them?"[5] The release of the White House tapes exposed several other critical comments, mostly on the predominance of Jews in media and entertainment, with the implication that this was something bad but which could not be discussed in the open.

And on go the comments, into recent times. Mathematical genius John Nash said, "the root of all evil, as far as my personal life is concerned…are Jews".[6] Chess genius and half-Jew Bobby Fischer was critical of them his whole life, particularly so in a series of radio interviews from the 1990s through his death in 2008. In 1999 he railed against "world Jewry":

> They invented the Holocaust story. There's no such [thing].[7]
> … They've been pulling this shit from time immemorial about persecution. They're a filthy, lying, bastard people.
> … *Study the history.*

---

[4] In Dinnerstein (1994: 232-233).

[5] "Tapes reveal Nixon's prejudices again," ABC News (21 Mar 2002).

[6] In Nasar (1998: 326).

[7] In reality, they did not literally "invent" the Holocaust, but small elements of truth were highly magnified, false inferences were reached, and inconvenient details were covered up. Again, see Dalton (2020) for details.

Indeed—the very purpose of the present work. Fischer's critique intensified in 2001 after the 9/11 attacks, which he called "good news":

> I applaud the act…the US and Israel have been slaughtering Palestinians for years. Robbing and slaughtering for years and treating everyone like shit. Now it is coming back at the US.

His proposed solution was to "arrest all the Jews, execute hundreds of thousands of the Jewish ringleaders, and apologize to the Arabs for the killing…"[8]

Even within the past decade or two, notable figures continued to speak out—including Mel Gibson, Helen Thomas, Rick Sanchez, John Galliano, Gary Oldman, Charlie Sheen, Hank Williams Jr., Kanye West, Kyrie Irving—only to find themselves slandered, unemployed, or otherwise punished. Between media, corporate leadership, and government, American Jews can deliver a "1-2-3 knockout punch" to any prominent person who dares challenge their dominance. One can only hope that principled, strong-willed individuals will continue to come forth, and continue to shed the light of truth upon the more pernicious aspects of global Jewry.

As I noted at the start of this book, it has now grown to the point where former Malaysian Prime Minister Mahathir Mohamad could rightly say, "Today the Jews rule the world by proxy," via their dominance over American policy and the American war machine. With enormous wealth at their disposal, access to the highest levels of government, and their virtual monopoly over Western media, Jews have a tremendous (though not unlimited) ability to shape events to their liking. From the first Iraq war in 1990, to their probable role in the 9/11 attacks, to the 2003 Iraq war, to the war against Afghanistan, to the Ukraine-Russia war, Jewish influence impacts millions of people, for the worse.

Reviewing the Big Picture

The picture portrayed in this book demonstrates the persistently malicious character of Jews throughout time and across Western Civilization.

---

[8] Transcript taken from online source: www.anusha.com/fischer1.htm.

There are, of course, many other important historical figures that one could mention, who likewise had critical assessments. For example, in 1584, the Italian Renaissance philosopher Giordano Bruno called the Jews "such a pestilential and leprous species, and one so dangerous to the public, that they deserve to be exterminated before birth"; indeed, "the Jews have proven to be the excrement of Egypt".[9] In 1858, French socialist Pierre Proudhon described Judaism as a "mercantile and usurious parasitism," adding: "the Jew remains a Jew, a parasitic race, an enemy of labor".[10] In the late 1860s and early 1870s, Russian anarchist and anti-Marxist Mikhail Bakunin had several critical comments. In a letter of 1869, he wrote:

> Long before the Christian era, their [the Jews'] history had already sent them in an essentially mercantile and bourgeois direction, and it is for this reason that, seen as a national group, the preeminently from the work of others... I know that in speaking out my intimate thoughts on the Jews with such frankness, I expose myself to immense dangers. Many people share these thoughts, but very few dare to express them publicly, for the Jewish sect, which is much more formidable than that of the Catholic and Protestant Jesuits, constitutes a veritable power in Europe today. It reigns despotically in commerce and banking, and it has invaded three-quarters of German journalism and a very considerable part of the journalism of other countries. Then woe to him who offends them![11]

And then, even more explicitly, Bakunin attacked the entire Jewish ethos in a letter of late 1871:

> Himself a Jew, Marx has around him, in London and France, but especially in Germany, a multitude of more or less clever, intriguing, mobile, speculating Jews, such as

---

[9] First quotation in Bein (1990: 713); also found in Bruno (2004: 196). The second quote is from Bruno (2004: 251).

[10] In Hart (2007: 69).

[11] "To the citizen editors of Le Reveil" (October 1869).

Jews are everywhere: commercial or banking agents, writers, politicians, correspondents for newspapers of all shades, with one foot in the bank, the other in the socialist movement, and with their asses sitting on the German daily press—they have taken possession of all the newspapers—and you can imagine what kind of sickening literature they produce.

Now, this entire Jewish world, which forms a single profiteering sect, a bloodsucker people (*ein Blutegelvolk*), a voracious collective parasite (*einzigen fressenden Parasiten*), closely and intimately united not only across national borders but across all differences of political opinion—this Jewish world today stands, for the most part, at the disposal of Marx and at the same time at the disposal of Rothschild. I am certain that Rothschild, for his part, greatly values the merits of Marx, and that Marx for his part feels instinctive attraction and great respect for Rothschild. … Jewish solidarity, that powerful solidarity that has maintained itself through all history, united them [both].[12]

Even the few truly honest Jews recognize in themselves such vices. Around 1900, Zionist leader Aaron David Gordon observed that "the Jewish people are…sick and diseased in body and soul." He attributed this to the fact that "we are a parasitic people. We have no roots in the soil; there is no ground beneath our feet. And we are parasites not only in an economic sense but in spirit, in thought, in poetry, in literature, and in our virtues, our ideals, our higher human aspirations".[13]

Another famous Russian, Pyotr Stolypin, wrote the following sometime in 1911, the very year that he was assassinated by a Jewish radical, Dimitri Bogrov:

It is important that racial characteristics have so drastically set the Jewish people apart from the rest of humanity as to make them totally different creatures who cannot enter into

---

[12] "Supporting documents: Personal relations with Marx." Partially reproduced in Wheen (1999: 340).
[13] In Sternhell (1998: 47-48).

our concept of human nature. We can observe them the way we observe and study animals, we can feel disgust for them or hostility, the way we do for the hyena, the jackal, or the spider, but to speak of hatred for them would raise them to our level. ... Only by disseminating in the popular consciousness the concept that the creature of the Jewish race is not the same as other people but an imitation of a human, with whom there can be no dealings—only that can gradually heal the national organism and weaken the Jewish nation so it will no longer be able to do harm, or will completely die out. History knows of many extinct tribes. Science must put not the Jewish race but the character of Jewry into such condition as will make it perish.[14]

Into World War Two, American poet Ezra Pound took great objection to Jewish involvement in the war, and in particular to their active and causal role. The so-called democratic nations of the West, he said, had been hijacked by Jewish special interests and were pushing a war-hysteria in order to benefit themselves. In a particularly striking line published in 1939 in the *Japan Times*, Pound wrote, "Democracy is now currently defined in Europe as 'a country run by Jews'".[15] This seems to be truer today even than during the war, and it has profound implications for our current love of 'democracy' as the greatest of all political systems.

*****

Such comments are, again, echoes of countless past rebukes. The most biting ones continue to ring in our ears: "a plague infesting the whole world" (Claudius); "an accursed race" (Seneca); "hatred of mankind" (Tacitus); "a den of devils" (Luther); "a republic of cunning usurers" (Herder); "cringing in misfortune, insolent in prosperity" (Voltaire); "borrow with deceit, and repay confidence with theft" (Hegel); "prosperous parasites" (Ross); "plastic demons of decay" (Wagner, Goebbels); "planetary master criminals" (Heidegger). And perhaps worst of all,

---

[14] In Vaksberg (1994: 6).
[15] In Tytell (1987: 257). Pound was not wrong; for more on the intricate Jewish role in WW2, see *The Jewish Hand in the World Wars* (Dalton 2025b).

Voltaire's warning: "deadly to the human race." Such damning assessments by some of history's most luminous thinkers cannot be dismissed; they demand action.

And through it all, Jews still find it incomprehensible that they are disliked. There seems to be an almost congenital inability to grasp why non-Jews view them with such contempt—and have done so for millennia. When pressed for an explanation, they put it down to mental illness, psychological disorder, or outright evil. Jewish commentators have labeled critics as "rigid, repressed, infantile, narcissistic, hostile, ... paranoid, irrational, aggressive, and prone to violence".[16] If only it were so simple.

Jewish ultra-Zionist Alan Dershowitz has a related analysis in his book *Chutzpah* (1991). He spends one or two pages contemplating our central question: "How does one understand…the virulent anti-Jewish statements of intellectuals throughout history?" He then cites a pathetically brief list of names, including some—like Edgar Degas, Alexander Pushkin, Thomas Edison, and Pierre Renoir—that did not warrant even a single mention here.[17] Yes…how to explain it? Dershowitz has his answer:

> The answer to the question 'why?' probably lies more in the realm of abnormal psychology than in any rational attempts to find understandable cause in history, or economics. Anti-Semitism is a disease of the soul, and diseases are best diagnosed by examining those infected with them. (113)

What an outrageous conclusion. All those great minds of history—far more than he names or even realizes—are little more than mentally ill, "diseased in the soul," simply because they find reason to critique the Jews. If there are grounds to find any "abnormal psychology" in all of this, it is in a Jewish psyche that repeatedly offends against non-Jewish humanity, over and over, in such a grotesque manner.

---

[16] Jaher (1994: 12); recall the longer passage cited in Chapter One.

[17] To be fair, he also mentions by name several individuals—Tacitus, Diderot, Kant, Wagner, Mencken, Dreiser, Shaw, Adams, Wells, Ford—that I did examine. But with so little in the way of elaboration, and almost no direct quotations, we are expected to take him at his word that the cited individuals were pathological anti-Semites.

The only rational point of agreement here can be to examine those individuals…yes, *their actual words, in full, in context, and in light of the broader and more persistent historical trends*. Maybe then we shall better understand this enduring phenomenon of anti-Jewish thought.

Perhaps the most telling admission comes from Jewish journalist Neil Baldwin. In his 2001 work *Henry Ford and the Jews*, he describes in the Afterword his shock—shock!—at discovering that so many famous men of history truly detested his race:

> [G]rowing up in the New York City of the 1950s, attending an elite prep school and then an East Coast college in the 60s, being Jewish never felt that "different"… Writing *Henry Ford and the Jews* therefore sent me into intellectual shock. I was obligated, for the first time in my mature life as a writer, to become familiar with as much of the documented record of two millennia of Jew-hatred as I could stomach. I was embarrassed to realize…that I had difficulty believing what I read about the extreme degrees to which Jews had been reviled and marginalized as a matter of course in European society from medieval times. As the pages of early drafts of my manuscript came cascading out of the laser printer, I found myself shaking my head in disbelief, incredulous at what I had just written, thinking, "This can't be true… This just *can't* be true." (2001: 325)

For poor Baldwin, this shocking fact "undermines my faith in behavioral logic," so incomprehensible is it to him. Meanwhile, the rest of us can only shake *our* heads in wonder at such blindness—as we contemplate a world in which such types of men do not hold sway over humanity.

CHAPTER 10

SOME OBJECTIONS REFUTED

Having now gone through the long history of anti-Jewish criticisms, I trust that the broader conclusion is clear: Jewish maliciousness and malevolence are deeply inbred in the Jewish people, such that persistent problems have recurred throughout all of history and in a variety of cultures; these same negative characteristics are ubiquitous in global Jewry today; therefore, non-Jewish societies must take the firmest actions possible to reign in Jewish power, to compensate peoples and nations for past damage (at Jewish expense), and to mitigate any future harm. This conclusion is well-attested by a vast number of observers, oftentimes among the most brilliant minds of their day.

For many, this is a shocking conclusion; various reactions are natural and understandable. For example, one may say,

> "I don't see these bad characteristics in the Jews I know. Or at least, not to a greater degree than in people generally. Jews today are not like that; in fact, I know two or three who are very honest, friendly, and nice."

This response is understandable but misguided, for several reasons. First is the obvious fact that it can be difficult to even know when you are dealing with a Jew. This is especially true given that Jews have, for centuries, gone to great lengths to hide their ethnicity. Surnames are a rough guide, but are subject to change and in many cases are ambiguous. Also, one can easily overlook mixed-race Jews, or those who may have strong family connections, such as a Jewish spouse or in-laws. Physical appearances can be deceiving; many Jews look White, but they are not.[1] And this problem has become worse in recent years thanks to the prevalence

---

[1] A full discussion of this topic would take me too far afield. Suffice to say here that 'White' can be plausibly defined as a Caucasian of indigenous European origin, which unconditionally excludes Jews. But many Jews will declare themselves as White, when convenient, simply to hide the truth.

of plastic surgery—especially to deal with that nasty 'Jewish nose.' Furthermore, Jews will use the old religion/ethnicity ploy to their advantage; secular Jews will say "I'm not Jewish," meaning religion, when in reality that fact is irrelevant. When it comes to personality, mindset, and values, Jewish ethnicity—i.e. genetics—is what really matters.

Second, all population subgroups have a wide variability in traits, even those traits with a strong genetic component. The fact that there may be some 'decent' Jews is to be expected. But history shows that the decent few are outnumbered by the pernicious many.

Third, the Jews 'you know' are likely not the most malevolent ones—those at the top of the Jewish wealth and power hierarchy. Spend some time with a Harvey Weinstein, a Chuck Schumer, or a Rahm Emanuel, and you'll get the idea.

Fourth, most people are not placed in conflict with Jewish attitudes or values on a day-to-day basis, and thus do not feel the brunt of Jewish action. The apologist reader should first take a public stand against Israeli genocide in Palestine, Israeli apartheid in Israel itself, against foreign aid to Israel, or challenge the Holocaust story, before proclaiming Jewish beneficence.

Finally, and perhaps most significantly, Jews today can afford to be magnanimous. At least in the major Western nations, Jews hold dominant influence; they are 'riding the whip hand,' as they say, and thus have no need at present to agitate, as they have in the past. Hence their negative qualities often work below the visible surface of society. This is certainly true in the United States, and also to a lesser degree in the UK, France, Canada, and Australia. Other nations have more unique but still related situations. All of Europe is effectively under control of the US, especially the NATO countries; they are unable to deviate in any significant way from policy specified by the American Jewish Lobby. Additionally, Germany is in the grip of a Holocaust-guilt ideology, and thus is doubly subservient to Jewish interests. India shares common cause with Israel in opposition to Islam. And in Russia, many of the so-called oligarchs—those billionaire nouveau-capitalists who hold sway over much of the economy—are Jewish.[2] Throughout the West and much of the rest

---

[2] Of the "seven bankers" that dominated Russia pre-2000, six were Jews; see "The richer they come..." (*Guardian*, 2 Jul 2007). More recently, of 10 Rus-

of the world, Jews need only maintain the status quo. It takes only one insolent Jew to set a policy, and then the rest simply follow along with implicit support. When Jews have the upper hand, it's easy for them to 'get along, go along.' And all the while, the truth about Jewish power and Jewish action remains safely hidden from view.

Ultimately, much of the American (and thus Western) public has been, in effect, brainwashed by Jewish-inspired media to accept the Jewish agenda. Multiculturalism, free-market capitalism, ubiquitous advertising and marketing, representative democracy, unrestrained immigration, notions of human equality, ruthless economic competition—all these work to Jewish advantage, and nearly all Westerners accept them as good, desirable, and necessary. This, despite the fact that *none* of these things have roots in classical Western civilization. Even our *Judeo-Christian* background—which is in truth a wholly Jewish construction—establishes sympathy to the Jewish cause. Thus, when Jewish values or characteristics are promoted in media, film, television, or governmental policy, most people don't even recognize them as such, let alone their pernicious consequences. Most of us are brainwashed to think Jewish, to a greater or lesser degree, and we therefore do not see it for what it is. This is one of the great tragedies of the 21st century.

*****

I can anticipate a few other objections at this point. First:

> "All this is pure hate speech. You're a hater, and everybody hates a hater."

Setting aside the illogic of 'hating a hater,' I would first point out that hating injustice is nothing evil. Only the unjust hate those who fight against injustice. Furthermore, there is a great irony here in that Jews themselves are world-class haters—the champion haters of all time, in fact. It is a typical Jewish tactic to take their own shortcomings and project them onto others. So, if you don't like hate speech, you can start with the Jews.

---

sian oligarchs with financial ties to Donald Trump, at least five are Jews ("Know your oligarch," *Ha'aretz*, 23 May 2018).

But more to the point, 'hate speech' is a favored label that Jewish groups deploy against their opponents. This, along with 'anti-Semitism' and 'White supremacy,' are their preferred slanders. The latter terms attempt to paint the person as morally deficient, but it also alerts other Jews (and non-Jewish sycophants) that the individual is willing to confront Jewish hegemony and hence that they should take appropriate action. The 'hater' label, however, is more effective because it (now) is backed by force of law. Jews cannot yet prohibit anti-Semitism because it is too narrow; but they can outlaw hate speech because it sounds more generic. And they can get blacks, Muslims, and Hispanics to buy in as well. It is quite a trick: getting other minorities, whom the Jews deeply detest, to fight on behalf of Jewish interests. This, in addition to getting many White liberals, whom the Jews also deeply detest, to fight on behalf of Jewish interests. In any case, we must be alert—anywhere we hear talk about the evils of hate speech, Jews are not far behind.

There is a second objection:

> "You don't like the Jews, but others don't like the Hispanics, the Muslims, or the blacks. Why aren't they targeted? And if we allow action against Jews, what's to stop others from taking similar actions against virtually any other group? Then it's total chaos."

If there is a central lesson from this book, it is that *Jews are different*: ethically, racially, socially, religiously, morally. For over 2,000 years, commentators have observed that the Jews are unlike any other people. They alone hate mankind; they alone are "the chosen"; they alone proclaim the right to rule over nations; and as a people, they excel all others in greed, deceit, arrogance, malevolence, and criminality. By their own profession, they are different. I say: Take them at their word. A people as uniquely different as the Jews require different rules; they are a special case in world history. There is no comparable argument, and certainly no basis in history, to enact any such policies against other ethnicities.

And then a third possible claim:

> "Why punish all the Jews, when only a few, at most, are
> truly guilty of certain crimes? Why not just the ringleaders,
> the bad ones?"

This is perhaps the hardest to accept. Of course, we could deal harshly
with just the richest, or the most corrupt, or the most malevolent. But it's
very hard to determine who are the actual worst of the lot, given the
complexity of human action. Even anonymous, mid-level Jews cause
significant damage. Certainly we could tax or financially penalize only
the richest ones, or expel only the convicted criminals. But the basic
problem here is that this does not get to the root of the problem. If, say,
we imprisoned or expelled the worst 20%, things might improve for a
while. But soon enough, there would emerge a new batch of domineering
Jews, and the problems would start again. This is the lesson of history.
No amount of pleading, reasoning, or cajoling seems to work with this
"chosen" people. They need to be identified, quarantined, penalized, and
at worst, expelled—as I elaborate a bit below. Two thousand years of
trouble and strife point to no other conclusion.

There is a fourth possible concern:

> "It's hard to believe that the Jews could really be a single,
> collective parasite, a bloodsucker people, as Bakunin said.
> People just aren't like that."

Just because *you* aren't like that, or your *race* isn't like that, doesn't
mean that another race can't be like that. Every human ethnic group has
unique and distinctive features; that's what makes them an ethnic group.
Among these features can be some very malicious or unpleasant characteristics—at least, when viewed from the outside. The fact that dozens of
very smart men have, over the centuries, found this to be true strongly
suggests that there is a real basis in fact here, and that non-Jews ought to
take it into account when dealing with Jews.

Here is a fifth objection, this one more thoughtful and insightful:

> "Jews are not the cause of our decay, they are a symptom. Only a corrupted and weakened people would allow Jews to dominate in the first place. It's like someone who neglects or abuses their body and then wonders why they get attacked by germs. Jewish domination is an indication that we are socially and politically ill, and that we need to take action to regain health."

Arguably true. Without doubt, any society that has been overtaken by a foreign minority needs to deeply reexamine its fundamental laws, values, and policies. If a given nation cannot do this, and remains chronically dysfunctional, then perhaps they deserve their fate. Nations that are unable to muster the will to sanction or expel those doing it harm don't deserve to exist. A case could be made that any Jewish-dominated nation should simply go under, dissolve, disband. Then the majority people might have a chance to start anew, at a smaller scale, learning the painful lessons of history.

Picking Cherries?

But there is yet another important possible objection to my study: that I have "cherry-picked" only the worst examples or the worst quotations from history, thereby painting a false or misleading picture of Jewish malevolence. Here are the exact words of one incensed critic:

> The sickening story that unfolds is an exercise in antisemitic poison. In typical conspiratorial strategy, the author produces a memo [quotation] to underscore a point, leaving behind the 999 memos that negate his argument. The power of a particular person is exaggerated because he is Jewish, whilst the non-Jews that surrounded him are covered in invisible ink. It is easy to distort history. Ten thousand politicians, millions of quotes—and if you just pick the ones that suit you, you can create anything you want to.

Well said! But completely wrong. As I noted above, the Jews constitute a unique situation in world history—both by their own accounting and by that of independent observers. For most races or groups, there are, indeed, a range of views, from highly negative to gushingly positive. So, why not the Jews? Are there not many positive opinions of Jews over the ages? And what if I have "cherry-picked" only the bad views, the negative stereotypes, and left out the positive views?

But since the Jews are a unique situation, we should not be surprised to learn that *nearly all historical views have been negative*. Obviously there are many neutral, objective, or strictly factual statements about them over the centuries, but we can set those aside; they work neither for nor against my claim and thus it is not 'cheating' to leave them out. However, if in fact I have neglected many, perhaps *equally* many, or perhaps even *more*, favorable comments, then indeed I would have misled the reader.

However, I did not. Note, first of all, that even if I were proven to be wrong about this, and that brilliant commenters from past ages said even more wonderful things about Jews, *this still does not negate the claims made in this book*. My quotations are precise, accurate, and well-sourced; they cannot be disputed. The individuals cited here in fact actually held those views, and had good reason, at least in their own minds, to espouse them. Nothing changes this fact, even with a mountain of evidence on the other side.

In reality, though, there is no such mountain; there is no heap; to the best of my knowledge, there is not even a bare handful of positive remarks. This is especially true for ancient times. Recall the side remark by Margaret Williams in chapter three, where she observes that a favorable comment by Strabo constitutes "one of the few favorable treatments of Judaism to survive from Graeco-Roman antiquity." And by "few," she is being generous, as I will demonstrate.

But to the point: In my years of research, I have found only one academic scholar who even attempted to make the claim that ancient commentators had nice things to say about Jews: Louis Feldman, a now-deceased orthodox Jewish academic who taught at Yeshiva University in New York. His lifelong work is summarized in his book *Jew and Gentile in the Ancient World* (1993), and which attempts to defend the idea that "Judaism elicited strongly positive and not merely unfavorable responses from the non-Jewish population" of antiquity.[3] But does he succeed? A look at his book shows a substantial amount of preliminary and peripheral discussion, such that only one chapter—Chapter 7: "Attractions of the Jews: The cardinal virtues"—contains relevant and specific quotations. Let me, therefore, briefly run through his strongest claims from that chapter, in order to determine if my quotations need to be balanced by philosemitic views.

Feldman's chapter centers on the four classic virtues of antiquity: wisdom, courage, temperance, and justice. These can be found, explicitly, in Plato's *Republic*, circa 375 BC. He then throws in a fifth virtue, piety. He proceeds to run through a list of ancient quotations defending the five virtues in the Jews; half of the chapter is dedicated to 'wisdom,' and half to the remaining four. But more importantly, Feldman includes quotations issued by ancient Jews (mostly, Josephus) as well as by the non-Jews—but it is precisely the non-Jewish view that is in question here. Jewish opinions are all but worthless; it is no surprise that ancient Jews had good things to say about their fellow Jews. And yet Feldman treats these equally to the others. Thus, for present purposes, we can essentially dismiss half of his chapter as unremarkable and irrelevant.[4]

So let's look at the half that remains and pull out the strongest positive claims, starting with 'wisdom.' Feldman begins with the assertion that the great philosopher Pythagoras was an "admirer" (p. 201) of the Jews. But his only evidence is from the writings of the Jew Josephus, working some 600 years later. Josephus cites an obscure but real philosopher, Hermippus of Smyrna, who allegedly said that Pythagoras "introduced many points of Jewish law into his philosophy." This quotation is found nowhere else, and we know for certain that Josephus takes great pains—and even fabrications—to construct a rosy history of his Jewish people.[5] Thus the passage, which is only implicitly positive, cannot be trusted. This is typical of Feldman's "evidence" for Jewish virtues.

The next compliment, such as it is, comes from Theophrastus—the same man cited in Chapter One in his critique of Jewish human sacrifice.

---

[3] For his earlier efforts, see Feldman (1958; 1988; 1991).

[4] Seven of 14 sections in the chapter are dedicated to quotations by Jews.

[5] In his *Against Apion* (I.176-183), Josephus invents an entirely fictitious meeting between Aristotle and a "learned Jew," simply in order to impute a Jewish influence on the great philosopher.

In the same passage, Theophrastus refers to the Jews as "philosophers by race" (or "by birth"), which Feldman takes as a positive remark. He then cites a Christian Father, Clement of Alexandria (circa 200 AD), who claimed that the wisdom of Greek philosophy could also be found in the Hindus and the Jews.[6] But this again is dubious because the Christian Fathers had a strong incentive to find "wisdom" in the Jewish Old Testament and to devalue the "pagan" wisdom of the Greeks. And this is not to mention that Greek philosophy was put down on paper in the 400s and 500s BC, whereas the OT is not known to be documented before 270 BC; if anything, it is far more likely that the Jews drew from the Greeks than vice versa.[7] In sum, neither Jewish nor Christian sources can be trusted to provide accurate and unbiased claims about Jews.

Moving to Hecateus—again, cited above—Feldman cites a passage in which Hecateus refers to Jewish priest Ezechias as "an able speaker"; this Feldman sees as "a great compliment." Hardly; and even so, does this really provide any insight into the Jewish people?

Other of Feldman's "complimentors" are utterly obscure and likely fictious people. He cites pseudo-Lucanus, pseudo-Longinus, and pseudo-Ecphantus (p. 204), all who are claimed to "paraphrase Genesis" in their writings; again, this is what passes for laudatory remarks about Jews. Next we have the (real) Roman historian Pompeius Trogus, who "pays enormous tribute" to the biblical Joseph, calling him an "extraordinary talent" and "shrewd." Joseph, we might recall, allegedly conned his way into power in Egypt, exploited the masses, and accrued vast wealth in the process; we can call this "talent" and "shrewdness" if we like, but it certainly is no compliment.

Another criticism of the Jews, cited above, is that they have contributed nothing useful to society—with the implication that they are mere leeches, drawing off the creative powers of non-Jews. But even here, Feldman finds a silver lining. Rather than denying that the Jews have done nothing of importance, he turns it into a virtue: "lack of inventiveness" is "a laudatory trait in Herodotus"—the Greek historian who supposedly said of the ancient Egyptians that (according to Feldman) "no

---

[6] *Stromata*, book I, chapter 15.

[7] This is the precise contention of Russell Gmirkin; see his book *Berossus and Genesis, Manetho and Exodus.*

change had taken place in their nature, manners, or customs".[8] So he distorts the words of Herodotus to benefit the Jews. Feldman then adds that Plutarch wrote of the Spartans' outlook: "Foreigners inevitably bring with them into a country foreign notions, novel ideas lead to novel choices, and these in turn are bound to cause the development of a number of feelings and inclinations which clash with the euphony [harmony], as it were, of the existing political system".[9] An interesting quote, but again, nothing that can transform Jewish non-inventiveness into a virtue. Feldman, it seems, is a master of turning historical lemons into philosemitic lemonade.

Feldman continues on, in similar fashion, for several pages:

- Comments by Emperor Hadrian that all synagogue chiefs were also astrologers "might very well be regarded as a compliment" (p 214).

- One Vettius Valens referred to "the first Jew, Abraham" [?] as "most wonderful"—though of course, Abraham was the alleged precursor of several peoples, not only Jews.

- Pausanias referred to "a Hebrew Sibyl named Sabbe, who is said to have given oracles," and simply to name her as a Hebrew, says Feldman, "adds to her praise."

- The Greek philosopher Numenius (circa 200 AD) asserted a connection between Plato and Moses, and wrote "What is Plato but Moses speaking in Attic Greek?" This, says Feldman, is "a great tribute paid to the Jews" (p. 215). But it wrongly assumes that (a) Moses was an actual person, (b) an actual connection exists between the two, and (c) Moses' ideas preceded Plato's. And as before, the source for this is the highly dubious *Stromata* of Clement, the Christian Father.

---

[8] In reality, Herodotus said "nothing in Egypt was altered at these times [the past 11,000 years]—nothing growing in the earth or living in the river was any different, and there was no change in the course of diseases or in the ways people died" (II.142). How this translates into a Jewish virtue is a mystery.
[9] *Greek Lives*, Lycurgus, 27.

- Diogenes Laertius says that "some unspecified writers trace the Jews back to the same origins [i.e. the Magi]. This is a great tribute because the Magi were revered as wise men par excellence" (pp. 215-216). Unspecified writers?

- The anti-Semite Apion first criticized Jews as blind, lame, and diseased, and yet elsewhere he accepts that, in their Exodus, they traveled the harsh journey to Judea in only six days. Therefore, says Feldman, Apion "is actually complimenting the strength and courage of the Israelites" (p. 221). Again, lemons into lemonade; can anyone really see this as complimentary?

- By a similar distorted logic, Feldman turns that great critic of the Jews, Tacitus, into an admirer: Of the siege against Jerusalem, Tacitus stated that the Jews were fanatical fighters, showing "equal stubbornness on the part of men and women... [T]hey were more fearful of life than death." This "contempt for death" (Feldman) is turned into a virtue because certain Stoics had argued that death is nothing to fear.

- But "the greatest tribute...to the high ethical standards of the Jews," says Feldman, "is paid by Emperor Severus," circa 230 AD, who occasionally recalled sayings "from certain Jews or Christians." Severus allegedly expressed a version of the Golden Rule: "What you do not wish done to yourself, do not do to another" (p. 227). Feldman attributes this rule to Hillel the Elder, a Jewish scholar who lived around the time of Jesus; and therefore, it is yet another "compliment." But Feldman forgets (or ignores) that the "Golden Rule" actually dates back to Plato; if anything, Severus was praising Plato, not the Jews.[10]

"In sum," says Feldman, optimistically, "intelligent observers in antiquity would have found much to admire in Judaism—and in particular, in the great figures of the Bible as paragons of the cardinal virtues so dear to

---

[10] Plato: "no one should touch my property or tamper with it...; and if I am sensible, I shall treat the property of others with the same respect" (*Laws*, XI, 913a).

the ancients" (p. 232). *Would* have, *might* have…but did not. Obviously, one is bound to find a handful of marginally complimentary remarks, but that in no sense outweighs or offsets the overwhelmingly negative assessment by a large number of major critics. The reader is invited to read through Feldman's Chapter 7, and indeed his entire book; one finds almost exclusively such 'stretched,' implied, or imputed remarks as I have shown above. And this, I emphasize, is the *sole* researcher to claim positive remarks in ancient times.[11]

Thus, I trust it is clear that the Jews had few if any friends in the ancient world. Their religion instructed them to despise others (the Gentiles), and others in turn despised them. But the originating source was the Jews themselves: their religion, their worldview, their values. They believed that God promised them dominion over the Earth. They were willing to use and exploit non-Jews for their own purposes. And they were willing to kill, and to die, to achieve their ends.

So much for antiquity. Was the situation any better in the Middle Ages or the Renaissance? One searches in vain. In the Renaissance, a handful of noted thinkers, including Pico della Mirandola and Marsilio Ficino, made positive use of Jewish theology, but actual praises are scarce. Apart from them, no other major figures came forth to defend the Jews.

What about the Enlightenment—that resurgence of reason in Europe, spanning roughly from 1650 to 1800? No luck there either. As the Jewish scholar Eisenstein Barzilay explains:

> The age of Enlightenment was one in which deep-seated emotions and attitudes were often swept aside in the name of the lofty principles of reason. In its desire to inaugurate a new era in the history of mankind, the Enlightenment could not, without violating its own principles, ignore the Jews completely. The emergence of a new attitude toward them clearly marked a victory of reason over passion and prejudice, but this victory was never complete. In the final analysis, reason and emotions were still irreconcilable. Even devoted friends of the Jews such as Dohm, Mirabeau and

---

[11] The entire book can be found here: https://library.mibckerala.org/lms_frame/ eBook/Jew and Gentile, in the Ancient - Louis H. Feldman.pdf

Gregoire made it clear that theirs was merely a plea for a new experiment in a new historical setting… They took this liberal stand in the hope that, as a result, a new type of Jew would emerge, ready to abandon his Jewishness for the sake of becoming integrated in society. As far as the contemporary Jew, however, was concerned, there was no difference of opinion between Gregoire and Goethe or between Dohm and Michaelis and others. They all considered him degraded and his role in society pernicious. Ill-will toward him was displayed by all, even by his friends.

This almost universal, negative attitude toward the eighteenth-century Jew needs further scrutiny. Its main source must be sought in the basic fact that the Jews, in spite of their having been Europeans for so many centuries, were still considered, even by themselves, to be utter strangers. (1956: 252-253)

"Ill-will toward the Jew was displayed by all, even his friends"—this is a perfection summation of the situation. The "almost universal negative attitude" of the Enlightenment was matched by an "almost universal negative attitude" of the earlier Renaissance, which in turn was a continuation of the "almost universal negative attitude" of antiquity.

Obviously, there were always the occasional exceptions. During the Enlightenment, a few men, such as John Locke, argued that Jews should not be excluded from civil rights due to their religion; but this is hardly an endorsement of the Hebrews or their activities. There was sporadic praise for exceptional individual Jews, such as the philosopher Spinoza (1632-1677) or the composer Felix Mendelssohn (1809-1847), but this obviously does not transfer over to Jewry in general. And if we look into the 20th century, we find just one or two major non-Jewish thinkers who offered selective praise for Jews—but one of these was Karl Jaspers, whose wife, Gertrud Mayer, was Jewish! Hardly an unbiased observer.

In sum, the alleged preponderance of favorable commentary on Jews by non-Jews, for at least the past 2,000 years, simply does not exist in any substantial manner. The "cherry-picking" charge against the present study fails to hold up under examination. If the reader or any knowledgeable scholar doubts this, I invite him or her to do the research, compile the favorable commentary on Jews, and publish the results. Feldman has attempted this for ancient writers but failed miserably. Perhaps others can do better for more recent centuries; the world awaits.

Yes—But What to Do?

I can hardly complete this survey without at least a passing discussion of the practical consequences. This is obviously important because the Jewish apologist may say at this point:

> "So what? All this history and criticism is meaningless and pointless. The fact is that we have thousands or millions of Jews in our country today. They're here. We just have to live with them. So there's nothing we can do."

But this is far from true. There are several phases of action that one could reasonably pursue, if one were willing to take the Jewish Question seriously. History provides us with many examples, more or less successful, for dealing with the Jews. Here, I will examine seven possibilities: *educate*, *identify*, *isolate*, *quota*, *penalize*, *tax*, and *evacuate*. Let's briefly look at each in turn.

Educate: There exists a huge amount of public ignorance on the Jewish Question. And deliberately so. There is a concerted effort by media, government, schools, and universities to say nothing negative about Jews, and to completely avoid any critical history. Thus, we must make a conscious effort to educate ourselves and the broader public. We should discuss these topics at every relevant occasion, utilizing the Internet and social media as needed to disseminate the truth—including the truth exposed in the present work. And we must have no doubts: *this is the truth*. Jews have had a justified and well-warranted negative image for centuries, even millennia. Many of our bravest and most brilliant thinkers have told us so, in no uncertain terms. There is no ambiguity here, no 'two sides,' no dispute. The harshly critical words are well-documented and indisputable facts. And in the present day, the dominant Jewish role in media, Hollywood, finance, academia, and government is another unquestionable truth. As a first step, we need only make these truths known.

Identify: Few people recognize prominent Jewish individuals as Jews. Some are relatively obvious, either through their occupation or social role, their life story, or their name. But the vast majority of influential Jews escape public notice, and this largely accounts for their ability to dominate various aspects of modern society. Hence a second task would be to call them out. Jews should be 'outed' at every occasion. Every story, article, report, or communication on them should include some such identification.

There are several ways to do this, from subtle to overt. One can be blunt—"the Jew Mark Zuckerberg"—but this comes off as sounding rude and offensive, for some reason (why is it not equally rude to say "the Pole Nicolaus Copernicus" or "the Italian Giordano Bruno"?). Internet-savvy people sometimes use clever notation, like (((Michael Dell))) or collectively, the (((mainstream media))), which works with some readers but is cryptic to others. Alternatively, one can invent new forms: Much as American congressmen are identified by party and state—for example, Paul Ryan (R-WI)—we could adopt a parallel nomenclature. Hence, something like: Bernie Sanders (J-VT); or more concisely, Jake Tapper (J) or Wolf Blitzer (J). Half-Jews might have this: Rachel Maddow (J/2). Those with a Jewish spouse (s) or child (c) could be identified thusly: Paul McCartney (J/s), or Donald Trump (J/c). It need not be too complicated; even these few designators would cover the vast majority of Jews, and would bring an unprecedented level of clarity to the situation, if widely used.

Isolate: Prominent Jews and Jewish-dominated industries could be sanctioned, through a process of severing of business ties, consumer boycotts, and denial of rights to conduct or expand their activities. There could be coordinated efforts to deny them profits, publicity, and power, and this might begin to weaken their stranglehold over most Western nations today. 'Clean' institutions and businesses could declare themselves as such, and would benefit thereby. It need not be absolute; evidence of freedom from Jewish domination should be sufficient. Eventually there might need to be a certification process of some sort, as we do in other industries, but this is certainly achievable.

Quota: If nothing else, it is grossly unfair and unjust that a small minority of any kind should have massively disproportionate wealth and power, in any country. Even if we want to say that they 'earned' it somehow, that still does not offset the many injustices associated with such a situation. If Jews are overrepresented, then many other groups are necessarily underrepresented. Thus a reasonable action would be to implement Jewish quotas in all fields, not only for the sake of fairness but also to limit the temptation and ability for harm.

In the US, for example, given that Jews are a less than 2% minority, they could be immediately restricted to, say, 4% or 6% representation in media, Hollywood, government, academia, and business. This still allows for double or triple overrepresentation, so it can hardly be considered unfair. Imagine if just one of every 20 films were Jewish-produced or -directed; or if only one out of every 20 talking heads on CNN or MSNBC were Jews; or if only one out of every 20 university professors were Jews; or if Jews controlled only 5% of American wealth rather than 50%. American society would be very different, and vastly better, than it is today.

Penalize: The cost inflicted on global humanity by Jewish activities over past centuries has been incalculable. We could scarcely begin to recoup these costs. But Jews have immense financial assets that could be seized, and this would be a start. For example, in the US alone, there is reason to believe that the six million American Jews possess or control an astonishing $80 trillion in assets.[12] Half of this could be immediately seized without reducing them to poverty. Funds could then be used to pay off *completely* the multi-trillion-dollar US national debt, and furthermore to issue substantial compensation—say, $50,000—to every American man, woman, and child. Just imagine the far-reaching, life-changing benefits if every American family of four received $200,000, tax-free, from a new "Gentile compensation fund." Similar calculations could be done in every country in which Jews predominate. This is not a fantasy; such things have happened in the past, and they could happen again if we had the collective will to do so.

---

[12] The US has about $160 trillion in personal wealth, and based on the fact that Jews constitute about half of the wealthiest Americans, we can infer that they own or control about half the total wealth.

<u>Tax</u>: Assets are one thing; income is something else. In order to prevent a return to massive Jewish wealth, and to cover on-going expenses of accommodating Jews, a Jew-specific tax could be implemented. This, as we know, is an ancient idea, originating in the *fiscus Judaicus* of the Roman Empire.[13] If, say, an incremental 20% or 30% tax were levied on Jewish income, this would certainly inhibit obscene accumulation of wealth, and it would provide substantial additional income for public works that have been badly-neglected under years of Jewish dominance.

<u>Evacuate</u>: Perhaps most contentiously, nations may have to consider revoking citizenship and expelling their Jews. If the pernicious qualities cited in this book are truly endemic, as they appear to be, then there is no other long-term solution. The lesson of millennia is this: Wherever Jews number more than a fraction of a percent of the populace, these malignant tendencies become manifest. Like incorrigible criminals, they—collectively—simply cannot help themselves. And so, like criminals, they may well need to be excluded from civil society. Obviously, this does not mean that literally all Jews are criminals; but it does mean that, in any sufficiently large population, that a disproportionate share will become criminal types. And not just low-grade criminality, as we might see in Black populations, but rather high-level, society-wide, deeply-corrupting criminality—the kind that will eventually destroy the social fabric.

Fortunately, since 1947, we have an option for them: Israel. Jews everywhere could, at first, be incentivized to move there, then firmly pressured, then ultimately compelled. This is hardly a cruel fate. Israel is a wealthy and prosperous nation, one that could easily accommodate the 14 million Jews worldwide. That state welcomes all Jews as immediate citizens; so, let it have them. With that abundance of Jewish skill, talent, and ability, Israeli society would surely flourish—assuming, that is, that Israel could manage to live a peaceful and just existence with their Arab neighbors.

Other nations, now devoid of their Jews, would likely flourish as well. This is not mere speculation; we have numerous historical examples of positive results. England expelled its Jews in 1290 and remained Jew-free for over 350 years, during which time it experienced the golden

---

[13] See Chapter Two.

age of the Elizabethan era and England's rise to a position of global dominance. All the Jewish expulsions of Renaissance Europe coincided with a flowering of culture and creativity. And even more dramatically in National Socialist Germany, which began to encourage Jewish emigration in 1933, and in six short years, by 1939, had risen from destitution to a world power. It happened before, many times; it can happen again.

Such is my briefest sketch of some of the options at hand. Note that these are not sequential actions; any combination can happen simultaneously. A concerned society could act on any or all of these phases immediately, to varying degrees. We have had to tolerate centuries of Jewish influence and domination; time to try a century or two without.

Closing Thoughts

If I should hazard some final conclusions here, three come to mind. First is that the evident persistence of these complaints against Jews, across millennia and over diverse nations and societies, is indicative of a real, objective, underlying cause—namely, personal and sociological Jewish traits that undoubtedly have a large genetic component. Where Jews appear, so do these problems. The form and intensity of their manifestation may be cultural or environmental, but the existence of the problematic characteristics is largely fixed, indicating a racial or genetic basis.

Second, the astonishingly disproportionate power and influence of the Jews seems due, in large part, to the corruptibility of those gentiles in power. We know all too well the moral fallibility of others, but it never fails to surprise at how easily, and how completely, people will compromise themselves for the wealth and power offered by the Jews. And it's not simply a matter of something like, say, prostitution, which comes at the expense of oneself; rather, it is a deeply criminal sort of corruption, as when one sells out one's own people or one's entire nation, or ruins whole economies, or damages the global environment, or commits mass murder, or any number of equally heinous crimes, simply for personal gain. The *Judenknechte* must be exposed, and held accountable.

Third is the amazing pliability of the public at large, and the relative ease with which the so-called democratic masses are manipulated and, as I said, brainwashed. To accomplish this, dominant control of media is essential. From the 1870s in Europe and the 1890s in America, Jews have held increasingly influential positions in press, radio, theater, and television—either as owners or managers (or both).[14] In the past four decades, this control has been almost complete. And the public seems either to not know, or not care. Perhaps the masses are content to let Jews run their lives. Or perhaps they are in denial about the modern-day *Judenfrage*—"it's not the Jews, it's the Republicans/Democrats, or the liberals/conservatives, or the unions, or the Muslims, or the poor..." The few who bother to dig into the matter know better, but they can do almost nothing about it. Clearly the situation will have to get much worse before the masses 'awake' (as the Germans used to say).

This also explains why we in the United States are so anxious to push our uniquely Jewish-American form of democracy on the rest of the world—a particularly toxic blend of globalism, laissez-faire capitalism, multiculturalism, inclusionism, and moral relativism, all backed by a high-tech infrastructure. It is precisely these conditions that are most favorable to Jewish-American interests, and it is these conditions that allow optimal manipulation of peoples and nations. There is a reason why Hitler and other National Socialists opted for nationalism, self-sufficiency, ethnocentrism, and anti-Semitism as their guiding policies. They knew that this would work—and it *did* work—until the Jewish-dominated nations conspired against them.

Thus my brief analysis will have to suffice. It is always a risky and speculative proposition to draw conclusions about the future from history. But one thing is certain. If by chance you should find yourself, dear reader, being critical of the Jews, know this: you are in good company indeed.

---

[14] Again, see Dalton (2020).

BIBLIOGRAPHY

Adams, H. 1905. *Mont-Saint-Michel and Chartres*. Houghton Mifflin.

Adams, H. 1969. *Letters of Henry Adams*, vol. 2. Houghton Mifflin.

Atzmon, G. et al. 2010. "Abraham's children in the genome era." *American Journal of Human Genetics* 86: 850-859.

Bachrach, B. 1977. *Early Medieval Jewish Policy and Western Europe*. University of Minnesota Press.

Baldwin, N. 2001. *Henry Ford and the Jews*. PublicAffairs.

Barzilay, I. 1956. "The Jew in the literature of the Enlightenment." *Jewish Social Studies* 18.

Bauer, B. 1852. "The present position of the Jews." *New York Daily Tribune* (7 June).

Bauer, B. 1958. *The Jewish Problem* (H. Lederer, trans.). Hebrew Union College.

Bauer, B. 1978. "The capacity of present-day Jews and Christians to become free" (M. Malloy, trans.). *Philosophical Forum* 8(2-4).

Bein, A. 1990. *The Jewish Question*. Basic Books.

Bendersky, J. 2000. *The Jewish Threat*. Basic Books.

Bischoff, E. 1929/2023. *The Book of the Shulchan Aruch*. Clemens & Blair.

Blake, W. 1982. *The Complete Poetry and Prose of William Blake*. University of California Press.

Bloom, H. 1998. *Shakespeare*. Riverhead.

Boatwright, M. 2008. "Hadrian," in *Lives of the Caesars* (A. Barrett, ed.). Blackwell.

Bonaparte, N. 1898. *New Letters of Napoleon I* (M. Lecestre, ed.). D. Appleton.

Brenner, L. (ed.). 2002. *51 Documents: Zionist Collaboration with the Nazis*. Barricade.

Bruno, G. 2004. *Expulsion of the Triumphant Beast*. University of Nebraska Press.

Carmi, S. et al. 2014. "Sequencing an Ashkenazi reference panel supports population-targeted personal genomics." *Nature Communications* 5:4835.

Carroll, J. 2001. *Constantine's Sword*. Houghton Mifflin.

Cavadini, J. 1999. *Augustine through the Ages*. W. Eerdmanns.

Chamberlain, H. 1899/1968. *Foundations of the 19th Century*, vol. 1. H. Fertig.

Chazan, R. 2016. *From Anti-Judaism to Anti-Semitism*. Cambridge University Press.

Chrysostom, J. 2025. *Homilies Against the Jews*. Clemens & Blair.

Cunningham, W. 1896. *The Growth of English Industry and Commerce*. McMaster.

Dalton, T. 2009. "Nietzsche on the Jews." On-line: www.theoccidentalobserver.net.

Dalton, T. 2010. "Nietzsche and the origins of Christianity." On-line: www.theoccidentalobserver.net.

Dalton, T. 2016. *The Holocaust: An Introduction*. Castle Hill.

Dalton, T. 2020. *Debating the Holocaust* (4th ed.). Castle Hill.

Dalton, T. (ed.) 2022. *Classic Essays on the Jewish Question: 1850 to 1945*. Clemens & Blair.

Dalton, T. (ed.) 2023. *Protocols of the Elders of Zion: The Definitive English Edition*. Clemens & Blair.

Dalton, T. 2025. *The Holocaust: 100 Questions and Answers*. Clemens & Blair.

Dalton, T. 2025b. *The Jewish Hand in the World Wars*. Clemens & Blair.

Dalton, T. (ed.) 2025. *Classic Essays on the Jewish Question* (vol. 2). Clemens & Blair.

Delaney, G. 2024. *The Monsters of Babylon* (2 vols.). SSPress.

Delaney, G. 2025. *The Sumerian Swindle*. SSPress.

Dershowitz, A. 1991. *Chutzpah*. Little, Brown.

d'Holbach, B. 1770/1813. *Ecce Homo!* D. I. Eaton.

d'Holbach, B. 1772. *Good Sense*. W. Stewart.

d'Holbach, B. 1771/1920. *Superstition in All Ages*. P. Eckler.

Dinnerstein, L. 1994. *Anti-Semitism in America*. Oxford University Press.

Disraeli, B. 1852/1969. *Lord George Bentinck*. Gregg.

Dreiser, T. 1933a. "Letter to Hutchins Hapgood." *The American Spectator* (10 Oct).

Dreiser, T. 1933b. "Letter to Hutchins Hapgood." *The American Spectator* (28 Dec).

Dreiser, T. 1959. *Letters of Theodore Dreiser*, vol. 2. University of Pennsylvania Press.

Duffy, M. and Mittelman, W. 1988. "Nietzsche's attitudes toward the Jews." *Journal of the History of Ideas* 49.

Dutch, O. 1940. *Hitler's Twelve Apostles*. R. M. McBride.

Eliot, T. 1934. *After Strange Gods*. Harcourt, Brace.

Emerson, R. 1929. *Complete Works*. Houghton Mifflin.

Entine, J. 2012. "Jews are a 'race,' genes reveal." *Forward* (11 May).

Falk, G. 1992. *The Jew in Christian Theology*. McFarland.

Feldman, L. 1958. "Philo-semitism among ancient intellectuals." *Tradition* 1(1): 27-39.

Feldman, L. 1988. "Pro-Jewish intimations in anti-Jewish remarks cited in Josephus' *Against Apion*." *The Jewish Quarterly Review* 3-4: 187-251.

Feldman, L. 1991. "The enigma of Horace's thirtieth sabbath." *Scripta Classica Israelica* 10: 87-112.

Feldman, L. 1993. *Jew and Gentile in the Ancient World*. Princeton University Press.

Ford, H. 1922/1998. *My Life and Work*. Ayer.

Ford, H. 2024. *The International Jew: The Definitive Edition* (two volumes; T. Dalton, ed.). Clemens & Blair.

Gabba, E. 1984. "The growth of anti-Judaism or the Greek attitude toward the Jews," in W. Davies and L. Finkelstein, (eds.), *Cambridge History of Judaism*, vol. 2. Cambridge University Press.

Gibbon, E. 1788/1974. *The History of the Decline and Fall of the Roman Empire*, vol. 2. AMS Press.

Gilbert, M. 2007. *Churchill and the Jews*. Henry Holt.

Gmirkin, R. 2006. *Berossus and Genesis, Manetho and Exodus*. T&T Clark.

Goebbels, J. 1948. *The Goebbels Diaries: 1942-1943* (L. Lochner, trans.). Doubleday.

Goebbels, J. 2024. *Goebbels on the Jews: The Complete Diary Entries, 1923 to 1945*. Clemens & Blair.

Gruen, E. 2011. *Rethinking the Other in Antiquity*. Princeton University Press.

Hart, M. 2007. *The Healthy Jew*. Cambridge University Press.

Hawthorne, N. 1856/1962. *English Notebooks*. Russell and Russell.

Hegel, G. 1975. *Early Theological Writings* (T. Knox, trans.). University of Pennsylvania Press.

Herder, J. 1968. *Reflections on the Philosophy of the History of Mankind*. University of Chicago Press.

Hertzberg, A. 1968. *The French Enlightenment and the Jews*. Columbia University Press.

Hitler, A. 2022. *Mein Kampf* (2 vols; T. Dalton, trans.). Clemens & Blair.

Hitler, A. 2024. *Hitler on the Jews* (T. Dalton, ed.). Clemens & Blair.

Hood, J. 1995. *Aquinas and the Jews*. University of Pennsylvania Press.

Jaher, F. 1994. *A Scapegoat in the New Wilderness*. Harvard University Press.

James, H. 1968. *The American Scene*. Indiana University Press.

James, H. 1996. *Complete Stories, 1892-1898*. Library of America.

Jefferson, T. 1905. *The Writings of Thomas Jefferson*, vol. 10. Thomas Jefferson Memorial Association.

Johnson, P. 1987. *A History of the Jews*. Harper.

Joyce, A. 2021. "Namatianus and the sullen Jew." On-line: www.theoccidentalobserver.net.

Kant, I. 1960. *Religion within the Limits of Reason Alone* (T. Greene, trans.). Harper.

Kant, I. 1967. *Philosophical Correspondence* (A. Zweig, trans.). University of Chicago Press.

Kant, I. 1978. *Anthropology* (V. Dowdell, trans.). Southern Illinois University Press.

Kant, I. 1979. *Conflict of the Faculties* (M. Gregor, trans.). Abaris.

Kant, I. 1997. *Lectures on Ethics* (P. Heath, trans.). Cambridge University Press.

Katz, J. 1980. *From Prejudice to Destruction*. Harvard University Press.

Lazaridis, I. et al. 2014. "Ancient human genomes suggest three ancestral populations for present-day Europeans." *Nature* 513(7518): 409-413.

Leopold, D. 1999. "The Hegelian anti-Semitism of Bruno Bauer." *History of European Ideas*, 25.

Levy, R. 1991. *Anti-Semitism in the Modern World.* D. C. Heath.

Lindbergh, C. 1970. *The Wartime Journals of Charles A. Lindbergh.* Harcourt, Brace.

Lindemann, A. 1997. *Esau's Tears: Modern Anti-Semitism and the Rise of the Jews.* Cambridge University Press.

Linder, A. 1987. *The Jews in Roman Imperial Legislation.* Wayne State University Press.

Luther, M. 1902. *The Table Talk of Martin Luther* (W. Hazlitt, trans.). G. Bell and Sons.

Luther, M. 1955. *Luther's Works*, vol. 54. Concordia.

Luther, M. 2025. *On the Jews and Their Lies.* Clemens & Blair.

Markish, S. 1986. *Erasmus and the Jews.* University of Chicago Press.

Martial. 1897. *Epigrams of Martial* (G. Bohn, trans.). G. Bell.

Marx, K. 1976. *Capital*, vol. 1 (B. Fowkes, trans.). Penguin.

Marx, K. 1978. "On the Jewish Question." In *The Marx-Engels Reader.* Norton.

Mencken, H. 1930. *Treatise on the Gods.* Knopf.

Mencken, H. 1956. *Minority Report.* Knopf.

Mendes-Flohr, P. and Reinharz, J., eds. 2011. *The Jew in the Modern World.* Oxford University Press.

Michael, R. 2008. *A History of Catholic Antisemitism.* Palgrave.

Moran, W. (ed.) 1987/1992. *The Amarna Letters.* Johns Hopkins University Press.

Muller, J. 2002. *The Mind and the Market.* Knopf.

Nasar, S. 1998. *A Beautiful Mind.* Simon and Schuster.

Nation of Islam. 2017-2023. *The Secret Relationship between Blacks and Jews* (3 volumes). Latimer Associates.

Oliphant, L. 1880. *The Land of Gilead.* William Blackwood and Sons.

Olmstead, F. 1861. *Journeys and Explorations in the Cotton Kingdom*, vol. 1. Sampson Low.

Ostrer, H. 2012. *Legacy: A Genetic History of the Jewish People.* Oxford University Press.

Patton, G. 1974. *The Patton Papers*, vol. 2. Houghton-Mifflin.

Poliakov, L. 1965. *The History of Anti-Semitism*, vol. 3. Vanguard.

Rather, L. 1990. *Reading Wagner.* Louisiana State University Press.

Rosenberg, A. 1970. *Alfred Rosenberg: Selected Writings.* Cape.

Rosenberg, A. 1930/2001. *The Myth of the Twentieth Century* (T. Dalton, trans. and ed.). Clemens & Blair.

Ross, E. 1914. *The Old World and the New.* The Century Co.

Samuels, E. 1964. *Henry Adams: The Major Phase.* Belknap Press.

Schafer, P. 1997. *Judeophobia: Attitudes toward the Jews in the Ancient World.* Harvard University Press.

Schopenhauer, A. 1969. *World as Will and Representation*, vol. 1 (E. Payne, trans.). Dover.

Schopenhauer, A. 1974. *Parerga and Paralipomena* (E. Payne, trans.). Oxford University Press.

Seldin, M. et al. 2006. "European population substructure." *PLoS Genetics* 2(9): e143.

Shabetai, K. 1995. "The question of Blake's hostility toward the Jews." *ELH* 62.

Shaw, G. 1932. "Shaw's 'Shofar-Blast'." *The Literary Digest* (Oct 22).

Simon, M. 1996. *Verus Israel*. Vallentine Mitchell.

Smith, G. 1893/1894. *Essays on Questions of the Day*. Macmillan.

Sombart, W. 1911/1982. *The Jews and Modern Capitalism*. Transaction.

Stern, M. 1974. *Greek and Latin Authors on Jews and Judaism*, vol. 1. Israel Academy of Sciences and Humanities.

Stern, M. 1980. *Greek and Latin Authors on Jews and Judaism*, vol. 2. Israel Academy of Sciences and Humanities.

Sternhell, Z. 1998. *The Founding Myths of Israel*. Princeton University Press.

Stevenson, R. 1892/1906. *Across the Plains*. Scribner.

Suetonius. 1979. *The Twelve Caesars*. Penguin.

Tacitus. 1997. *The Histories*. Oxford University Press.

Tacitus. 2012. *Annals*. Penguin.

Teachout, T. 2002. *The Skeptic: The Life of H. L. Mencken*. HarperCollins.

Toaff, A. 2020. *Passovers of Blood*. Clemens & Blair.

Trawny, P. 2015. *Heidegger and the Myth of a Jewish World Conspiracy*. University of Chicago Press.

Truman, H. 1997. *Off the Record*. University of Missouri Press.

Twain, M. 1898. "Stirring times in Austria." *Harper's New Monthly Magazine* (March).

Twain, M. 1899. "Concerning the Jews." *Harper's New Monthly Magazine* (September).

Tytell, J. 1987. *Ezra Pound: The Solitary Volcano*. Anchor.

Vaksberg, A. 1994. *Stalin Against the Jews*. Knopf.

Wagner, R. 1881/1972. *Prose Works* (volume 6). Scholarly Press.

Wallace, M. 2003. *American Axis*. St. Martin's Press.

Washington, G. 1894. *Maxims of Washington*. Appleton.

Wells, H. G. 1922. *The Outline of History*. Macmillan.

Wells, H. G. 1933/1945. *The Shape of Things to Come*. Macmillan.

Wells, H. G. 1936. *Anatomy of Frustration*. Macmillan.

Wells, H. G. 1939. *Travels of a Republican Radical in Search of Hot Water*. Penguin.

Wells, H. G. 1939b. *The Fate of Homo Sapiens*. Longmans, Green.

Wells, H, G. 1971. *The Outline of History*. Doubleday.

Wells, H. G. 2005. *Tono-Bungay*. Penguin.

Wheen, F. 1999. *Karl Marx: A Life*. Norton.

White, A. 1892. "The truth about the Russian Jew." *Contemporary Review*.

Wilcox, R. 2008. *Target: Patton*. Regnery.

Williams, M. 1998. *The Jews among the Greeks and Romans*. Johns Hopkins University Press.

Wilson, H. 1941. *Diplomat Between Wars*. Longmans, Green.

Wistrich, R. 2010. *A Lethal Obsession*. Random House.

INDEX

www.ingramcontent.com/pod-product-compliance
Lightning Source LLC
Chambersburg PA
CBHW051147120626
46547CB00012B/981